XI'AN

A Note on Transliteration

In this book addresses are given in *Pinyin*. *Dajie* is a main thoroughfare; *lu* is a road and *jie* is a street; *xiang* is a lane or alley.

To help visitors getting about on their own, Chinese characters for names and addresses of hotels and restaurants are provided under 'Practical Information'. Names of all the sights, shops and other places described in the book are given in Chinese characters either under 'Useful Addresses' or in the index.

XI'AN

— ✵ —

Simon Holledge
Photography by Jacky Yip
Revised by
William Lindesay and Wu Qi

PASSPORT BOOKS
a division of *NTC Publishing Group*
Lincolnwood, Illinois USA

Published by Passport Books in conjunction with
The Guidebook Company Ltd

Library of Congress Catalog Card Number: 9809-3

This edition first published in 1993 by Passport Books, a division of NTC Publishing Group,
4255 W. Touhy Avenue, Lincolnwood (Chicago), Illinois 606-46-1975, USA, originally published by
The Guidebook Company Ltd © The Guidebook Company Ltd. All rights reserved. No part of this book
may be reproduced, stored in a retrieval system, or transmitted in any form, or by any means, electronic,
mechanical, photocopying or otherwise without the prior permission of NTC Publishing Group.

Grateful acknowledgment is made to the following authors and publishers for permissions granted:

Faber and Faber Limited for
Journey to a War by W H Auden and Christopher Isherwood © revised edition 1973 W H Auden and
Christopher Isherwood

Foreign Languages Press, Beijing for
Tu Fu: Selected Poems compiled by Feng Chih and translated by Rewi Alley

Kodansha International Ltd for
Lou-lan and Other Stories by Yasushi Inoue translated by Edward Seidensticker
© 1979 Kodansha International Ltd

RENDITIONS (The Chinese University of Hong Kong, Research Centre for Translation) No 23,
Spring 1985 for
'*The Long Longing*' by Li Bo translated by Moon Kwan

Hodder and Stoughton for
Alone on the Great Wall by William Lindesay © Hodder & Stoughton

Thames and Hudson Ltd, London for
China Diary by Stephen Spender and David Hockney © 1982 Stephen Spender and David Hockney

William Heinemann Limited for
Behind the Wall by Colin Thubron © 1987 Colin Thubron

Century Publishing Co, London for
China's Sorrow by Lynn Pan © 1985 Lynn Pan

Editor: May Holdsworth
Series Editor: Anna Claridge
Illustrations Editor: Caroline Robertson
Design: De•Style Studio
Map Design: Bai Yiliang

Photography by Jacky Yip
Front cover by James Montgomery; back cover by Wang Miao, Hong Kong China Tourism Photo
Library. Additional photography courtesy of: Gary Chapman 59; China Guides Series 26, 27, 149; Luo
Guoshi and Luo Lingbi 35; Simon Holledge 65; Yu Shi Jun 106–107; William Lindesay 31, 143; Wang
Miao, Hong Kong China Tourism Photo Library 8–9, 130; Yang Li Min, Hong Kong China Tourism
Photo Library 62; Luo Zhong Min 5, 14, 42, 43, 68, 69, 76–77, 119; Ingrid Morejohn 139; Wattis Fine
Art 89; Wei Wang Xiang, Hong Kong China Tourism Photo Library 84

Production House: Twin Age Limited, Hong Kong
Printed in Hong Kong by Sing Cheong Printing Co Ltd

Soldiers of Qin Shihuangdi's buried army

Contents

An Introduction to Xi'an   —David Bonavia

The city of Xi'an has been the capital of China for longer than any other—a total of some 1,100 years.

The magnificent archaeological and art discoveries in and around the city tell the tale of China's development from prehistorical times till the height of the imperial period. There have been so many astounding finds in the area that only a small proportion are as yet on view to the public, although a growing number of them are now being put on display.

Xi'an was at different times the capital of the Zhou, Han, Sui and Tang dynasties. Lying on the Wei River in Shaanxi Province, it commanded the approaches to central China from the mountains of the northwest. It was also the starting point of the old Silk Road along which Chinese merchandise was taken as far west as the Mediterranean.

The modern city is plain and business-like, but the narrow residential alleys and street markets bear the flavour of old China. Sections of the old city wall testify to Xi'an's strategic importance down the ages.

Easily accessible from Xi'an is Yan'an, where the late Chairman Mao Zedong's followers in the Communist Party built up their strength for the final confrontation with Generalissimo Chiang Kai-shek's Nationalist forces. Chiang was actually captured in his nightgown trying to escape from the hot springs resort near Xi'an, by a younger commander who wanted him to unite with the Communists and fight the Japanese—the famous Xi'an Incident of 1936.

Dubbed 'the land of kings and emperors' by Du Fu, China's most famous poet, Xi'an can trace its origins to the 11th century BC, when the rulers of the Zhou Dynasty set up Fenghao, a twin city made up of Fengjing and Haojing, about 16 kilometres (ten miles) southwest of the present site. The city was grid-shaped—a pattern which later became common in Chinese cities. It was said that nine carts could ride abreast on each of the 18 main roads of the grid.

In the eighth century BC, the Zhou Dynasty moved its capital downstream to Luoyang. A ruler of the Kingdom of Qin, in northwest China, established his capital at Xianyang, just north of Xi'an. In 221 BC the King of Qin conquered the other feudal kingdoms to become the First Emperor. Qin Shihuangdi, as he became known, imposed an early form of totalitarianism on China. He consolidated and extended the various sections of the Great Wall which was to keep out fierce northern tribesmen. He standardized the Chinese written language and even the span of cart axles. But his oppressive rule broke down when his son succeeded to the throne, and after a bloody civil war a rebel commander called Liu Bang established the Han Dynasty with its capital at the city which was now called Chang'an.

(preceding pages) Loess landscape of the Yellow Earth Plateau, northern Shaanxi Province

The Han Dynasty was a period of great cultural flowering and imperial expansion. Pottery, bronze and iron work, lacquer, precious metal, wall-painting and sculpture of a very high artistic standard survive in impressive quantities. Chang'an was three times the size of Rome at the time. Chinese and Roman soldiers may actually have crossed swords in central Asia, but this has not been proven.

Qin Shihuangdi died in 210 BC. In accordance with the custom of the time, it is believed, he had his ministers, family members, slaves and horses buried with him—but whether all of them were actually killed, as would have been normal a few centuries earlier, or whether some were buried later as they died naturally, is not clear. The main part of the tomb is yet to be excavated.

But pottery figures of soldiers and horses leave no doubt that the emperor wanted a bodyguard in the afterlife. There are estimated to be some 8,000 clay warriors, whose existence was discovered by some peasants digging a well in 1974. Each human figure differs from the other—or so it seems—and they are slightly larger than life-size. They wear a variety of uniforms and body-armour, though all have a flowing, knee-length robe, a turned-round lapel, and breeches. They wear their hair in elaborate topknots and sport moustaches. Some are kneeling in postures which suggest that they once held drawn bows of wood, now decayed. The whole tomb area covers nearly 57 square kilometres (22 square miles). There is an outer wall with four gates and an inner wall with five—two of them being on the north side. The figures are a fascinating direct link with the past over a period of 22 centuries.

In AD 25 the Eastern Han Dynasty removed the capital to Luoyang. From the third century there ensued a period of civil war and division of China into separate kingdoms, sometimes with rival claimants to the title of Emperor. But in 582 the founder of the Sui Dynasty, Yang Qian, restored the city as the capital. It was enlarged and improved and a famous Chinese poet wrote of it: 'Ten thousand houses look like a laid-out chessboard'. Merchants and tribute bearers from central and western Asia arrived with exotic products. But the new capital shortly fell to Li Yuan, who established the Tang Dynasty. The most famous imperial concubine in Chinese history, the beauty Yang Guifei, and the most powerful empress, Wu Zetian, inhabited the imperial palace in the Tang Dynasty. In its cultural achievements, the Tang outdid even the Han Dynasty, especially in poetry, painting, music, ceramics and calligraphy.

With the fall of the Tang Dynasty in AD 907, the capital was removed—after a period of civil war—to the city of Kaifeng in Henan Province in AD 960, and later, when the Jin Tartars invaded north China, to Hangzhou in the east. In 1295 the Mongols led by Kublai Khan conquered all China and established their capital at Beijing. The Ming Dynasty (1368–1644), while governing from Beijing, rebuilt the inner section of the city now called Xi'an, but it was never to be the capital again.

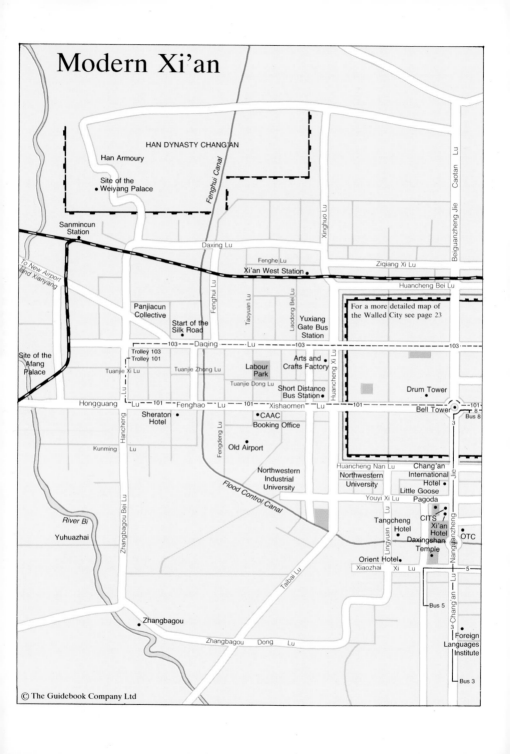

Modern Xi'an

HAN DYNASTY CHANG'AN

Han Armoury

Site of the
• Weiyang Palace

Fenghui Canal

Caotan Lu

Beiguanzheng Jie

Sanmincun
Station

Daxing Lu

Xinghuo Lu

Fenghe Lu
Xi'an West Station •

Ziqiang Xi Lu

To New Airport
and Xianyang

Huancheng Bei Lu

Fenghui Lu

Panjiacun
Collective

Taoyuan Lu

Laodong Bei Lu

Yuxiang
Gate Bus
Station

For a more detailed map of
the Walled City see page 23

Start of the
Silk Road

Site of the
Afang
Palace

Tuanjie Xi Lu

Tuanjie Zhong Lu

Labour
Park

Arts and
Crafts Factory

Huancheng Xi Lu

Drum Tower

103 — Daqing — — — Lu — — — — 103 — — — — — — — — — 103 —

Tuanjie Dong Lu

Short Distance
Bus Station •

Hongguang

Lu — 101 — Fenghao — Lu — 101 — Xishaomen — Lu — 101 — — — — Bell Tower

Hancheng Lu

Sheraton
Hotel •

Fengdeng Lu

• CAAC
Booking Office

Bell Tower

101
8
Bus 8

3

Kunming Lu

Old Airport

Northwestern
Industrial
University

Flood Control Canal

Huancheng Nan Lu

Northwestern
University

Chang'an
International
Hotel •
Little Goose
Pagoda

Chang'an Jie

Youyi Xi Lu

River Bi

Zhangbagou Bei Lu

Yuhuazhai

Lingyuan Lu

Tangcheng
Hotel •

CITS •
Xi'an
Hotel •
Daxingshan
Temple

Nanguanzheng

OTC

Orient Hotel •
Xiaozhai   Xi   Lu

Taibai Lu

Chang'an Lu

Nanguanzheng Lu

5

Bus 5

Zhangbagou •

3

Zhangbagou   Dong   Lu

• Foreign
Languages
Institute

Bus 3

© The Guidebook Company Ltd

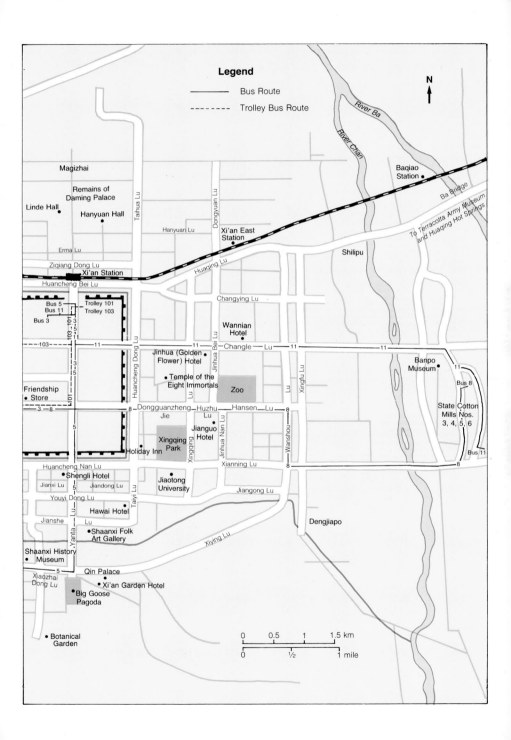

The main tourist attractions of today's Xi'an are the Ming-dynasty Drum Tower and Bell Tower near the city centre, the Shaanxi History Museum, Shaanxi Museum, the Big Goose and Little Goose Pagodas, the Great Mosque, the old city wall, the stone-age site at Banpo, the Famen Temple, and above all the pottery figures buried in the ground to guard Qin Shihuangdi's tomb.

Numerous other imperial tombs are known to exist, though they may have been despoiled by tomb-robbers and will take time to excavate. Yangling, the tomb of Han Emperor Jing, was discovered in 1991 during the construction of the highway linking Xi'an to the international airport in Xianyang. An army of archaeologists is now an integral part of any construction project, and new discoveries are expected as the Xi'an–Baoji expressway is being built.

Although the city is quite heavily industrialized, the Chinese Government has decided to give priority to excavation and restoration of ancient sites and buildings. Unfortunately much damage had already been done to the old city, which cannot be restored. Nevertheless, the once-magnificent city wall has now been carefully re-paired, and provides a spacious and open promenade around Xi'an for both citizens and visitors to enjoy.

Facts for the Traveller

Getting to Xi'an

Before the Second World War the few foreigners who made the arduous journey to Xi'an considered themselves adventurers rather than tourists. To reach their destination they had to travel to the end of the railway line in the neighbouring province of Henan, and then transfer to bumpy carts for a further journey of six days through 'bandit infested' country. The journey became easier when the railway reached Xi'an in 1934. A new station was built only in 1986. Today Xi'an has become the main communications centre for the northwest region of China.

BY AIR

Since 1 September 1991, when a new airport in the neighbouring city of Xianyang opened, air capacity to Xi'an has increased and ground service has improved.

Dragonair, the Hong Kong-based airline, recently inaugurated a round-trip service to Xi'an on Wednesday and Saturday. The Xi'an arm of CAAC, China Northwest Airlines, offers a direct service from Hong Kong four times a week— every Tuesday, Thursday, Saturday and Sunday—and now provides a service to Nagoya, Japan, on Tuesday, Thursday, Friday and Sunday. Daily flights are available to/from Beijing (1 hr 30 mins), Shanghai (1 hr 50 mins), Chengdu (1 hr 30 mins), Guangzhou (2 hrs 30 mins) , Chongqing (1 hr 50 mins) and Yinchuan (1 hr 40 mins). There are also air connections with Changsha, Dunhuang, Guilin, Kunming, Nanjing, Lanzhou, Taiyuan, Urumqi, Shenzhen, Zhengzhou, etc.

To reach Xi'an from Xianyang Airport take either a taxi (Rmb 100) or the airport bus (Rmb 5). From Xi'an to the airport the starting point for the airport bus is at China Northwest Airlines Booking Office (see Useful Addresses, page 142). Journey time on the new expressway is under one hour.

BY RAIL

Xi'an is on the main east–west railway that goes all the way from Shanghai to the Alataw Pass on the Xinjiang Autonomous Region border with Kazakhstan. A new Eurasian railway continues to Alma Ata, and then through several CIS republics before eventually ending up in Rotterdam.

Express trains arrive daily from Beijing (taking about 18 hours), and also from Shanghai, Chengdu, Chongqing, Guangzhou, Lanzhou, Nanjing, Qingdao, Taiyuan, Urumqi, Wuchang, and Zhengzhou. Travellers from Hong Kong can book sleepers

Swiss Efficiency

Sian is remarkable for its rickshaws. They have blue or white hood-covers, embroidered with big flowers, of an oddly Victorian design. We used the rickshaws a good deal, out of laziness, despite Dr Mooser's warning that their upholstery often contained typhus-lice. Typhus is one of the great scourges of Shen-si Province. One of Mooser's two colleagues, an engineer, went down with it soon after his arrival, but, thanks to an inoculation, the attack was comparatively slight.

Dr Mooser himself was a stocky figure, eagle-eyed with a bitter mouth and a smashed, rugged face. He wore a leather jerkin, riding-breeches, and big strapped boots. He rushed at life, at China, at this job, with his head down, stamping and roaring like a bull. The dishonesty and laziness of the average Chinese official was driving him nearly frantic. 'While I'm here,' he bellowed at his assistants, 'you are all Swiss. When I go away you can be Chinese again, if you like—or anything else you Goddam well please.'

Not that Mooser had much use for his countrymen either, or, indeed, for any Europeans at all. 'The Swiss are crooks, the Germans are crooks, the English are the damn lousiest crooks of the lot . . . . It was you lousy bastards who wouldn't let ambulances be sent to China. I have all the facts. I shall not rest until they are published in the newspaper.' With his colleagues he spoke Swiss dialect, or English—boycotting High German, the language of the Nazis.

Dr Mooser had established several refugee camps in Sian, as well as a delousing station. The refugees were housed in empty buildings. As soon as could be arranged they were sent off into the country and distributed amongst the neighbouring villages. There were about eight thousand of them in the city, including one thousand Mohammedans, who had a special camp to themselves. These people belonged mostly to the middle class of China—nearly all of them had a little money. The really poor had no choice but to stay where they were, and await the coming of the Japanese. The really rich were already safe in Hong Kong.

There was no doubt of Mooser's efficiency. The camps were well run, the floors and bedding clean, the children's faces washed, and there was hardly any spitting. Mooser was a great favourite with the children. Whenever he visited them his pockets were full of sweets. 'I had to sack three camp commandants in the first week,' he told us. 'They call me The Chaser.'

Mooser didn't quite know what to make of us—especially after he had heard from me that Auden was a poet. He had no use for poetry because 'it changes the order of the words'. While he was working in Mexico he was summoned to the bedside of an Englishman named David H Lawrence, 'a queer-looking fellow with a red beard. I told him: "I thought you were Jesus Christ." And he laughed. There was a big German woman sitting beside him. She was his wife. I asked him what his profession was. He said he was a writer. "Are you a famous writer?" I asked him. "Oh no," he said. "Not so famous." His wife didn't like that. "Didn't you really know my husband was a writer?" she said to me. "No," I said. "Never heard of him." And Lawrence said: "Don't be silly, Frieda. How should he know I was a writer? I didn't know he was a doctor, either, till he told me."'

Dr Mooser then examined Lawrence and told him that he was suffering from tuberculosis—not from malaria, as the Mexican doctor had assured him. Lawrence took it very quietly. He only asked how long Mooser thought he would live. 'Two years,' said Mooser. 'If you're careful.' This was in 1928.

W H Auden and Christopher Isherwood, Journey to a War, 1939

Dr Mooser and his two Swiss colleagues, of the League of Nations Commission, were advising the Chinese government on the prevention of infectious diseases.

through CITS (see page 21) for the 34-hour trip from Guangzhou. Luoyang, the historic 'Eastern Capital', is 387 kilometres (240 miles) east of Xi'an. The journey takes seven hours, and there are trains every day.

Hard and soft sleeper tickets can be bought in advance on the second floor of Xi'an Railway Station Ticket Office. The entrance is on the right-hand side, to the east of the station building alongside a left luggage office.

You can purchase tickets up to five days in advance of travel. During the peak season and at the Spring Festival (the lunar New Year holiday) you may have to wait five days for your train. At other times of the year, travel at two days' notice is possible. You can buy hard seat tickets at the last minute (the day of departure) from the ticket office on the ground floor of the Railway Station Ticket Office. Beware of hawkers selling cancelled invalid tickets.

Visas

Everyone must get a visa to go to China, but this is usually an easy, trouble-free process. Tourists travelling in a group are listed on a single group visa—a special document listing all members of the group—which is issued in advance to tour organizers. Individual passports of people travelling on a group visa will not be stamped unless specifically requested.

Tourist visas for individual travellers (those who are not travelling in a group) can be obtained directly through Chinese embassies and consulates, although some embassies are more enthusiastic about issuing them than others. Certain travel agents and tour operators around the world can also arrange individual visas. It is simplest in Hong Kong, where there are a large number of travel agents handling visa applications. Just one passport photograph and a completed application form are necessary.

Visa fees vary considerably, depending on the source of the visa, and on the time taken to get it. In Hong Kong, for instance, some travel agents can get you a tourist visa in a few hours, but it may cost around US$40 for one valid for three months, while one which takes 72 hours to obtain might cost just US$20.

The visa gives you automatic entry to all China's open cities and areas (there were 804 in 1992). Travel permits to certain areas of China, obligatory in addition to the visa, were dropped in 1986.

The mechanics of getting a business visa are much more flexible than in the past, particularly in Hong Kong. The applicant should have either an invitation from the appropriate Foreign Trade Corporation (several now have permanent representatives abroad), or from the organizers of a special trade fair or seminar. In Hong Kong, all

Drying red chillies

that is needed is a letter from the applicant's company confirming that he wishes to travel to China on business.

Regular business visitors are eligible for a multiple re-entry visa which may be obtained with the help of a business contact in China. Some Hong Kong travel agents can also arrange re-entry visas for clients—the cost might be around US$50–60. This type of visa may be for three or six months.

One-month extensions for 25 FEC can be arranged at the Division of Aliens and Exit-Entry Administration of the Xi'an Municipal Public Security Bureau close to the Bell Tower (see Useful Addresses, page 144).

Customs

A customs declaration form must be filled out by each visitor upon entry—the carbon copy of this form will be returned to you and must be produced at customs for inspection on departure from China.

Some personal possessions that you are asked to list on arrival—such as tape recorders, cameras, watches and jewellery—must be taken out with you when you leave. When you arrive you will be told at immigration which items these are, and they may be inspected by customs officials on departure from China.

Four bottles of alcohol, three cartons of cigarettes, unlimited film and unlimited medicines for personal use may be taken in. Firearms and dangerous drugs are strictly forbidden.

Money

CHINESE CURRENCY
The Chinese currency, which is sometimes referred to as Renminbi or Rmb, meaning 'people's currency', is denominated in *yuan* which are each divided into 10 *jiao*, colloquially called *mao*. Each *jiao* is, in turn, divided into 10 *fen*. There are large notes for 100, 50, 10, 5, 2 and 1 *yuan*, small notes for for 5, 2 and 1 *jiao*, and coins for 5, 2 and 1 *fen*.

CURRENCY CERTIFICATES
Foreign Exchange Certificates (FEC) were introduced in 1980. These were designed to be used instead of Renminbi by foreigners, Overseas Chinese, and Chinese from Hong Kong and Macau only, for payment in hotels, Friendship Stores, trade fairs,

and for airline tickets, international phone calls, parcel post etc. In actual practice, however, FEC became a sought-after form of payment anywhere, and a black market developed between the two currencies. In September 1986 the Chinese government announced its intention of phasing out FEC, but implementation seems to have been indefinitely postponed, and FEC remain in circulation.

FEC and Renminbi may be reconverted into foreign currency or taken out when you leave, but it is impossible to change them outside China.

FOREIGN CURRENCY
There is no limit to the amount of foreign currency you can bring into China. It is advisable to keep your exchange vouchers as the bank may demand to see them when you convert Chinese currency back into foreign currency on leaving China.

All the major freely negotiable currencies can be exchanged at branches of the Bank of China, and in hotels and stores.

CHEQUES AND CREDIT CARDS
All the usual American, European and Japanese traveller's cheques are acceptable. Credit cards can be used in a limited number of Friendship Stores, hotels and banks. You should check with your credit card company or bank before you rely on this form of payment for your purchases. Personal cheques are sometimes taken in return for goods which are shipped after the cheque is cleared.

TIPPING
Though it is still officially forbidden, tipping has appeared in major cities. Tourism staff (including drivers and guides) will generally welcome tips, if not always expect them.

Travel Agencies

There are a number of State-owned corporations which handle foreign visitors to China. The largest is China International Travel Service (CITS). Other large organizations providing similar services are China Travel Service (CTS), China Youth Travel Service (CYTS) and Overseas Travel Corporation (OTC).

These agencies offer a comprehensive service covering accommodation, transport, food, sightseeing, interpreters, in addition to special visits to schools, hospitals, factories and other places foreigners might be interested in seeing (see Useful Addresses, page 142).

Holidays

In contrast to the long calendar of traditional Chinese festivals, modern China now has only three official holidays: May Day, 1 October (marking the foundation of the People's Republic of China) and Chinese New Year, usually called Spring Festival in China itself, which comes at the lunar new year.

Climate and Clothing

Xi'an's climate is much drier and cooler than that of southwest or southeast China, and less extreme than that of Beijing. In American terms, the climate is similar to that of Wyoming. The Qinling Mountains to the south of the Wei River valley shield Xi'an from the southeastern monsoon, which brings much rain and considerable humidity to the neighbouring province of Sichuan. Annual precipitation is only 530–600 millimetres (21–24 inches). Most of the rainfall occurs in July, August and September.

Spring is the best season, with the city at its most beautiful under clear, bright skies. Summer begins in May, and is usually fine and sunny. The hottest month is July, when noon temperatures may reach over 38°C (100°F). Late summer and early autumn is cooler and can be overcast. Late autumn is usually fine, and winter is dry and cold with a little snow. At night during winter temperatures usually drop well below 0°C (32°F).

In mid-summer only the lightest clothing is necessary. In mid-winter thermal underwear and multi-layered clothing add to comfort.

XI'AN TEMPERATURES

	Average	High	Low		Average	High	Low
Jan	-1.3°C (29°F)	5.1°C (41°F)	-5.5°C (22°F)	Jul	26.7°C (80°F)	34.0°C (93°F)	22.5°C (72°F)
Feb	2.1°C (36°F)	8.0°C (46°F)	-2.4°C (28°F)	Aug	25.4°C (78°F)	31.5°C (89°F)	20.9°C (70°F)
Mar	8.0°C (46°F)	14.7°C (58°F)	2.7°C (37°F)	Sep	19.4°C (67°F)	25.0°C (77°F)	15.5°C (60°F)
Apr	14.0°C (57°F)	21.5°C (70°F)	8.6°C (47°F)	Oct	13.6°C (56°F)	20.0°C (68°F)	8.9°C (48°F)
May	19.2°C (67°F)	27.7°C (82°F)	13.8°C (57°F)	Nov	6.5°C (44°F)	12.4°C (54°F)	2.3°C (36°F)
Jun	25.3°C (78°F)	32.8°C (91°F)	19.0°C (66°F)	Dec	0.6°C (33°F)	6.2°C (43°F)	-3.9°C (25°F)

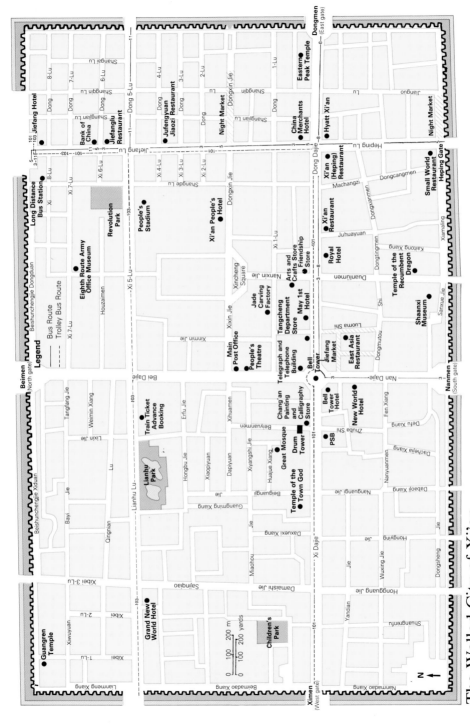

The Walled City of Xi'an

Getting around Xi'an

There are some fascinating areas within the city walls which are well worth exploring on foot. Particularly attractive for their old buildings are the streets around the Drum Tower and the Great Mosque as well as those near the South and West Gates and north and west of the Shaanxi Museum. Dong Dajie, the main shopping area, is another good place to stroll, with its large department stores and wide sidewalks. Xi Dajie is more compact and has dozens of small shops with a variety of intriguing items.

There are several **trolleybus** lines in the city and a number of **bus** lines, some of which extend into the newly developed urban areas. Public transport is cheap but can prove difficult unless you have full directions written out in Chinese or a basic knowledge of the language. **Taxis** are available at the hotels, and can also be hailed in the streets. There are usually taxis waiting at all the major places of interest to tourists. The drivers are supposed to charge by the kilometre travelled, but in practice they often charge a lump sum which is higher than the kilometre fee would be. It is best to establish the price before you set out, and to have your destinations written down in Chinese since taxi drivers rarely speak English.

If you prefer to cycle around Xi'an, you can rent a **bicycle** for Rmb4–5 a day from one of the bicycle rental shops in the city centre. One convenient location is near the gate of the People's Hotel (see page 135), where there are a few small shops.

Here is a suggested cycling route around Xi'an from the gate of the People's Hotel: Bell Tower–Drum Tower–Southern Gate of the City Wall–Small Goose Pagoda–Shaanxi History Museum–Big Goose Pagoda (Tang Dynasty Arts Museum and Qin Palace)–Eighth Route Army Museum. The distance covered is about 15 kilometres (9.3 miles). Another cycling route can be found alongside the interior of the city wall (see page 120).

Many of Xi'an's major sights are a long way from the city, but CITS and other travel agencies offer **tours** by comfortable Japanese buses to some of these places. The cheapest alternative for independent travellers is to join up with a Chinese tour group; ticket sellers for such tours are usually found plying their trade to bus passengers arriving at Xi'an Railway Station. Tours to the Terracotta Army Museum depart between 8 am and 11 am. Buy tickets (Rmb20) from a small kiosk between Jiefang Hotel and Dong Ba Lu.

There are three different tours available:

EAST ROUTE Lintong and Terracotta Army Museum, Huaqing Hot Springs and Banpo;

NORTHWEST ROUTE Qian Ling, Zhao Ling and Xianyang Museum;

WEST ROUTE Famen Temple and Mao Ling.

They can also be easily arranged at all major hotels for Rmb20–60 a day. Public buses go to most sightseeing places as well.

Those who prefer to arrange their own itinerary can hire a taxi for the day (Rmb100–200). With your own transport a worthwhile two-day trip may be made to the sites on the West and Northwest routes. You can take your taxi from Xi'an and go to Zhao Ling, Qian Ling and Famen Temple on the first day. After an overnight stay at the Huaxing Hotel in Qilizhen, Xingping County, the following day you can visit Mao Ling and the Xianyang Museum, returning to Xi'an on the Xianyang–Xi'an expressway.

Shopping

Earlier this century Xi'an was known for its curio shops stocked with antiquities of the city. Today, however, you would be lucky to find anything very old; most antiques in these shops date from the Qing and Republican periods. Curio-hunters may well come across some genuine, though small, antiques in the shops at the major sights, notably the Terracotta Army Museum, the Qin Tomb, Qian Ling Tombs and the Great Mosque. Enthusiastic salesmanship may win you over but be wary of the centuries-old dates that are blithely tossed about and bargain hard. It is worth having a quick look at the **Xi'an Antique Store** on Dong Dajie.

Shaanxi's folk crafts are thriving with the rapid increase of tourism in Xi'an. Hawkers cluster round every site visited by tourists, selling brightly coloured patchwork waistcoats and shoulder bags, embroidered children's shoes, hats and toys, shadow puppets, and amusing painted clay ornaments decorated in brilliant primary colours. Buying in the free markets can be much more fun than in the established arts and crafts shops, but be prepared for some fierce bargaining. Prices should be considerably less than in the official stores. The **National Folk Art Gallery** at 16 Yanta Lu (open 9.00 am–6.30 pm) accepts all the major credits cards but sells little of real quality or interest.

Embroidery is one of Shaanxi's richest traditional skills that is gaining recognition elsewhere; some of the more distinctive items crop up in hotel souvenir shops and Friendship Stores in other parts of China. There are children's patchwork waistcoats, predominantly red, and decorated with some, or all, of the 'five poisonous creatures'—toad, snake, centipede, lizard, scorpion—in the belief that the process of sewing the forms onto the waistcoat will nullify the creatures' evil powers. Embroidered cylindrical cotton pillows, with an intricately decorated tiger's head at each end, are also common. These are favourite gifts to babies when the first month of life is celebrated. Tiger motifs often appear on other children's clothes and shoes, since the tiger can readily devour evil spirits. Its eyes are usually wide open and staring to help deflect evil influences away from the wearer.

Painted clay toys, originally from the nearby city of Fengxiang, were traditional gifts for festivals, weddings and birthdays. Now available in many of the free markets and souvenir shops in the city, they can be bought for a few *yuan*. These toys are often in the form of tigers, sometimes covered with flowers or butterflies, and are predominantly red and green to symbolize prosperity and happiness. Other popular subjects are comical monkeys and chubby children.

Child's appliquéd vest featuring four of the 'five poisonous creatures'

Shadow puppets, cut out of semi-transparent hide and painted in bright colours, are another speciality of Xi'an. The puppet's flexible joints allow it—in skilled hands—to somersault expertly, or engage in armed combat. The characters depicted are usually from traditional folk tales.

Chinese stone rubbings are a very appropriate souvenir of China's former capital since Xi'an has the country's best collection of steles, or inscribed stone tablets, most of them in the Forest of Steles (see page 110). The rubbings of memorials, calligraphy, pictures and even maps are produced by laying paper on top of a stele, and then pounding it with a tightly-wrapped ink-filled cloth formed into a kind of mallet. It is often possible to see this being done, either at the Forest of Steles or at a handicraft factory. An expert job from a famous stone can cost hundreds, even thousands, of *yuan*. Rubbings of all prices are on sale almost everywhere around the city.

You may find it interesting to visit the workshops and showrooms of some small handicraft enterprises. Quality varies; none of the factories are particularly old but some of the craft techniques are worth seeing, and you will always be given a warm welcome. The **Cloisonné Factory** of Xi'an which employs some 400 workers is at 9 Yanta Lu, near the Big Goose Pagoda. The **Jade Carving Factory** of Xi'an is at 173 Xiyi Lu, round the corner from the Friendship Store, and has a retail outlet. Some

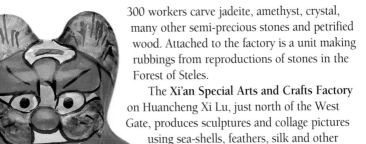

300 workers carve jadeite, amethyst, crystal, many other semi-precious stones and petrified wood. Attached to the factory is a unit making rubbings from reproductions of stones in the Forest of Steles.

The **Xi'an Special Arts and Crafts Factory** on Huancheng Xi Lu, just north of the West Gate, produces sculptures and collage pictures using sea-shells, feathers, silk and other material together with inlaid wood-work.

Other interesting items found most easily at the small shops surrounding major sights include local pottery for everyday use, basket-ware, papercuts, and micro-carvings on minute pieces of ivory no bigger than a grain of rice.

Fengxiang County painted clay tiger

The **Friendship Store**, an obligatory stop on many CITS tours, is in Nanxin Jie (open 9 am–7 pm), and carries all the usual items found in Friendship Stores throughout China. A selection of papercuts is worth looking out for. An elderly woman, Li Zhuying, is an expert on the ancient craft. She is at the store every morning after 10 am to show her skill and sell her own works. Reproductions of Xi'an's archaeological relics are on offer here as well; there are, for example, Qin soldiers of varying sizes, but it is worth noting that you can buy these replicas for far less at the Terracotta Army Museum itself. Although it is called the Friendship Store, the staff here are not that friendly.

Compared with the Friendship Store, the three-storeyed **Jianguo Hotel Friendship Shopping Mall** has a more varied stock and provides better service. Works of Huxian peasant painters (see page 58) are displayed on the second floor. On the same floor there is also an antique counter selling Ming and Qing antiques, for example porcelain, embroidered items and shadow puppets.

Many tourist shops sell Chinese paintings and calligraphy. Most of the work is by mediocre local artists, of which there are literally scores. The city's most famous artists are Luo Guoshi and his son Luo Liangbi, who specialize in painting local scenic spots (see page 35). Their work can be viewed at **Xi'an International Store**, Da Cien Temple branch inside the Big Goose Pagoda.

The **Jibao Art Treasures Store** in Nanxin Jie and **Wenbaozhai Store** on Yanta Zhong Lu are also worth looking at.

Replicas of Banpo pottery can be bought at the **Banpo Museum Retail Shop**.

The main shopping street is Dong Dajie, particularly the section between Nanxin Jie and the Bell Tower. The principal department store, the **Tangcheng Department Store**, is located on the north side of Dong Dajie, at the intersection with Luoma Shi. Carrying the most up-to-date products available to local Xi'an people, it is interesting to visit even if you do not plan to buy anything. Luoma Shi used to be where mules and horses were sold in ancient times, but the street has now become the biggest clothing market in Xi'an with fashionable stock from the export-orientated garment factories of the Special Economic Zones of Guangdong. Further along Dong Dajie are the **Foreign Languages Bookshop**, the **Xinhua Bookshop** (for publications in Chinese), and shops selling posters, clocks, sunglasses and an assortment of other products. There are also restaurants, snack-bars and fruit and vegetable stalls.

Just around the corner, and opposite the Bell Tower, is a Chinese opera costume shop supplying the municipal and county opera troupes of Shaanxi Province with embroidered silk costumes, elaborate head-dresses, hats, false beards and whiskers and odd props. There are many small shops like this on Xi Dajie.

A fascinating, newly-built, Qing-dynasty style **Ancient Culture Street** located next to the Shaanxi Museum, has many calligraphy and painting stores, cloisonné stores and folk art stores. It comprises the largest concentration of handicrafts and arts shops in the city and should not be missed.

Another important shopping area is around Jiefang Lu, within the northeast corner of the walled city. The biggest and best department store, **Minsheng**, is located here.

Oriental carpets from the western provinces of Xinjiang and Gansu, traditionally called Chinese Turkestan, can be found at the Friendship Store, the Jianguo Shopping Mall and other hotel shops. Prices are better here than in the larger Chinese cities like Beijing and Shanghai.

Food and Drink

In Xi'an the fare is generally plain and provincial, although good food is available if you search it out. Street-stall cooking is often better than that offered by the restaurants, which is itself better than the convenient but unexciting meals served by the hotels.

In country areas of Shaanxi Province (of which Xi'an is the capital) noodles and steamed bread are more popular than rice, and mutton is an important source of protein. Eating habits throughout the northwest of China have been strongly influenced by the Hui, Chinese-speaking Muslims who of course do not eat pork. Their food can be sampled at the stalls around the Drum Tower, especially in the early evening. The best-known, best-loved dish is called *kaoyangrou*, spicy barbecued mutton on skewers. Boiled mutton ravioli served in spicy sauce, *yangrou shuijiao*, sold by the bowl for one *yuan*, can be found in the same area.

The most popular local dish, also Hui in origin, is the hearty *yangrou paomo*. For the standard local price of about Rmb 2–3, a big bowl and two large baked flatbreads are provided. The customer breaks the bread into very small pieces and takes the bowl back to the kitchen where a mutton and vegetable soup, with noodles, is poured over the broken pieces of bread. It is difficult to describe the taste—perhaps something like haggis stew, noodles and digestive biscuits come closest to it!

At a relatively more sophisticated level, Xi'an has its own special delicacies served in some of the larger restaurants. Banquets start with a cold plate of *hors d'oeuvres* arranged in the shape of a phoenix, peacock or butterfly. Other dishes include fish in milk soup, served in a copper chafing dish (*guozi yu*), coin-shaped egg and hair vegetables (*jinqian facai*), sliced pig tripe and duck gizzard (*cuan shuang cui*), whole crispy 'calabash' chicken (*hulu ji*) and braised quail (*tiepa anchun*). Chinese wolfberry and white fungus in soup (*goupi dun yiner*) is a tonic, particularly good for the lungs.

Sweet dishes offered in ordinary restaurants tend to be sugary, starchy and filled with red bean, peanuts or *baihe*, lily bulb. A number of different cakes and biscuits are on sale, including crystal cakes (*shuijing bing*) and egg-thread cakes (*dansi bing*).

The leading brand of liqueur is called 'Xifeng', a colourless spirit made in Liulin Village, near Fengxiang, about 145 kilometres (90 miles) west of Xi'an. Another local drink is the yellow Osmanthus Thick Wine (*Huanggui choujiu*). Both are said to owe their origin to alcoholic drinks of the Tang period. Xi'an has a few varieties of its own beer, the best of which is aptly named 'Xi'an Beer'. 'Hans Beer' is also good.

Restaurants in Xi'an are generally open from around 10 am to 8 pm—but note that many will not serve guests without reservations after 7 pm.

There is a snack street in **Xiliu Lu** in the northeast of the walled city (opposite the Bank of China). You can have dumplings, noodles etc from 7 am–10 pm. *Yangrou suantang shuijiao* (mutton dumplings in spicy soup) is highly recommended. Such delicacies can be enjoyed at Muslim establishments which usually display a mirror inscribed with a pot and Arabic script (the pot being a symbol of Muslim cleanliness as it holds water for washing hands).

The standard charge for an ordinary meal for a foreigner is around Rmb 25 per head. Banquets are two or three times that figure.

Entertainment and the Arts

Xi'an is the home of several professional performing arts organizations serving both the city and the countryside. The city also has its own Conservatory of Music (at Daxingshan Temple Park), a provincial Opera School attached to the Institute of Opera in Wenyi Lu, and its own film studio (see page 32) near the Big Goose Pagoda.

The **Shaanxi Acrobatics Troupe**, which includes conjurors, is very popular with local people. Together with most of the various performing arts groups, this is based near Wenyi Lu, just south of the walled city. Close by is the building of the **Shaanxi Song and Dance Troupe**. This company is known for its vocal, orchestral and instrumental performances of both Chinese and Western music, including Western light classical, international folk and Chinese operatic pieces.

The **Xi'an Song and Dance Troupe** concentrates on Western ballet and Chinese traditional dance. Like the Shaanxi troupe it has its own orchestra. It is also located south of the walled city, at a small studio near Xiaozhai, although it performs in many different places. In addition, Xi'an has the **Shaanxi Puppet Group**, and a troupe specializing in Chinese traditional story-telling and comic dialogues.

There are eight big theatres in the city. The most important is the **People's Theatre** on Bei Dajie. This is mainly used for concerts, dancing and Beijing opera (performed by the Shaanxi Number One and Shaanxi Number Two Opera Companies).

If you have time to see only one artistic performance you should perhaps choose the celebrated local Qinqiang opera of Shaanxi Province itself.

China has over 300 forms of local theatre, and Qinqiang is one of the oldest, most vigorous and most influential of them all. It is almost certainly the original form of 'clapper opera', with which it is synonymous. In this style of Chinese opera, time is beaten with large wooden clap boards that look like oversize castanets.

Xi'an city has two Qinqiang companies. The drama is performed in local Xi'an dialect, with its own characteristic, rather loud, vocal style, accompanied by string instruments. It has its own conventions of costumes and make-up. Individual operas are often three or four hours long with rapidly developing plots using all the dramatic devices found in Shakespearean comedies—abrupt changes in fortune, mistaken identities, men dressed as women, women dressed as men, both as animals (notably predatory, acrobatic tigers). Drag parts in which comedians take off vulgar, meddlesome old ladies are often star roles.

Unfortunately, in the fast-changing China of the 1990s, Qinqiang is losing its popularity, especially amongst young people. The two Qinqiang companies have been forced to spend most of their year touring the countryside, where the farming communities still enjoy live operas. If you are interested, you should ask your guide

Poster for the film Judou, directed by Zhang Yimou

XI'AN FILM STUDIO

In 1985 a Chinese movie, *Yellow Earth*, was hailed as the most imaginative and original film shown at the London Film Festival that year. *Yellow Earth's* beautifully shot scenes of the loess landscape of Shaanxi, its innovative use of imagery and the bold political stance implicit in its theme of remorselessly unchanging peasant attitudes promised an exciting breakthrough in Chinese cinema.

This has not quite happened, although, for a time, there was a remarkable concentration of creative film directors in Xi'an.

Xi'an Film Studio, established in 1956, is housed in a group of semi-derelict warehouses on Xiying Lu near the Big Goose Pagoda—a good view of the site can be gained from the top of the Qin Palace film set.

Several of the so-called 'Fifth Generation' of film-makers (post-Cultural Revolution graduates of the Beijing Film Academy) flocked there in the early 1980s. Chen Kaige, the director of *Yellow Earth*, and Zhang Yimou, its cinematographer, both worked in Xi'an, although neither was officially employed by the city's film studio. During that period, the head of Xi'an Film Studio was Wu Tianming, and it was he who gave the young directors the support and encouragement to break out of the mould: while the studio continued to produce popular or politically correct films, it sponsored a few on the basis of their artistic potential rather than their mass appeal or propagandist content. Several of the pictures, after long deliberation by Chinese censors, secured international release. These include *Life*, based on a novella by Shaanxi-born writer Lu Yao; *River Without Buoys* (by the same director, Wu Tianming); *Wild Mountain*, directed by Yan Xueshu; *Big Parade* (directed by Chen Kaige, with Zhang Yimou as cinematographer); and *The Black Cannon Incident*, directed by Huang Jianxin.

Wu Tianming and Chen Kaige have since moved to the United States, but Zhang Yimou has remained in Xi'an, where he grew up. In recent years Zhang has become Xi'an Film Studio's most famous son, making a series of movies which have attracted a great deal of attention from world cinema circles. After making his debut as a director with *Red Sorghum* (voted best picture at the Berlin Film Festival), he has directed *Judou* (first Chinese film to be nominated for an Oscar), *Raise the Red Lantern* and *The Story of Qiu Ju* (winner of the Golden Lion Award at the Venice Film Festival in 1992).

to check the *Xi'an Evening News* to find out when performances are scheduled in the city and if so, where you can buy tickets.

A few hotels stage their own live entertainment. The Grand New World Hotel boasts a theatre which can accommodate an audience of 1,130 and on every odd-numbered evening has various performances such as an ancient-style dance, acrobatics, opera and ballet.

In the Xi'an Garden Hotel there is a Tang theatre, and a choice of two restaurants where you can taste French or Tang-dynasty court cuisine before you enjoy the show for US$25. The restaurant serving Tang-style dinners is called the Huaqing. Its most famous dish is Palace Fish (*Gongting xian yu*). Reservations are essential and should be made at the hotel's main reception desk by 2 pm. The after-dinner show will only go ahead if the audience numbers ten or more.

Both the People's Hotel (on every even-numbered evening) and the Tangle Palace (on every evening during the tourist season) put on shows featuring Tang-style dances.

Artists At Large

We had luncheon at a restaurant in Sian—in an upstairs room reserved for foreigners, with separate tables for groups of tourists. It was a large, light, airy, rather pleasant room. Our pretty local guide, while we were still sitting at table, asked David [Hockney] to do a drawing of her, which he obligingly did. Within a few minutes the waiter at our table stopped serving (there was a group of French tourists at the next table who seemed to be left unattended) and was standing over David watching the progress of his work. Soon other waiters appeared and, after them, sweating and smiling, the chef. David finished his drawing. He then fished into the enormous canvas bag which Gregory always carried round and drew out his Polaroid camera. He took the guide across the dining room to a window and photographed her, setting down the portrait he had just done, on another chair beside her, for comparison. By now the whole staff of the restaurant—or of the foreigners' section of it—was clustered by the window. David took a charming photograph of the chef—wearing his white chef's cap—flanked by two assistants.

After this, even outside the restaurant in the street, where there was a small crowd awaiting us, the citizens of Sian seemed particularly friendly, as though we were three Goons arrived there. We did look rather funny: David with the flat cap he nearly always wears, even indoors, his shirt with horizontal red stripes and his different coloured socks; Gregory with his Robin Hood jerkin with a kind of cape at the back; and me with my enormous feet. The Chinese, I noticed, were always looking at my feet and politely concealing their smiles.

Stephen Spender and David Hockney, China Diary

The Little Goose Pagoda, painted by Luo Guoshi and Luo Liangbi

Flora and Fauna

During the Tang Dynasty (AD 618–907) horticulture flourished in the capital Chang'an (present day Xi'an). One of its citizens was the most celebrated gardener of Chinese history, the hunchback 'Camel' Guo. He is supposed to have grown golden peaches and propagated lotus with deep blue flowers by soaking the seeds in indigo dye.

The inhabitants of the capital were especially proud of their tree peonies, which became something of a mania, and blooms were sold for huge sums in the Chang'an Flower Market. The most popular colours were pale pink and deep purple. Tree peonies had been cultivated from about the fifth century onwards, originally in either Shaanxi or Sichuan. (The plant did not reach Europe until 1789 when the first one was found a home in London's Kew Gardens.) The best peony garden was at Da Cien Temple, the temple of the Big Goose Pagoda (see page 90). It is no longer there today, but the **Xi'an Botanical Garden** (open every day 8 am–6 pm) has a small garden and is an excellent place to escape the crowds that fill most tourist sights. It is located on Cuihua Lu, south of the city, and can be reached by bus number 27 or by taxi.

In the second century BC, an envoy of Emperor Han Wudi (reigned 140–86 BC), who was sent to central Asia, brought the pomegranate tree back to China. Today, during the months of May and June, the hillsides around Lintong County, including the slopes of the Mausoleum of the First Emperor of Qin, are covered with the red and white pomegranate flowers. The fruit grown in Xi'an and especially Lintong, 15 kilometres (9 miles) to the east, is considered the best in the country, giving rise to the Chinese saying that 'When you think of Lintong, you think of pomegranates'.

The first attempt to catalogue the animals, birds and reptiles of Shaanxi according to Western science was made in 1908–9. Robert Stirling Clark of New York led an expedition of 36 men, including the ornithologist Arthur de C Sowerby of the Smithsonian.

Among some of today's rarest birds recorded by Sowerby were the pink, grey and white 'Chinese' ibises. These wading birds, members of the stork family, are properly called Japanese ibis, though they are called *toki* in Japan. The long-beaked birds are distinguished by the bright red colouring on the side of the head and legs. The adult grows to a length of about 77 centimetres (2.5 feet) head to tail.

These ibises were formerly spread throughout east and northeast China, Korea and Japan, but environmental changes in the 20th century have been disastrous for the species. They declined in numbers and disappeared altogether after 1964. By 1980 there were only two known pairs left in the world. These were at the Toki

Protection Centre on Japan's Sado Island. They had not reproduced for four years, and artificial incubation failed. Then, that same year, Chinese zoologists found two nesting pairs in Shaanxi, at Yangxian County in the Qinling Mountains. Three young were hatched that year in what is now the Qinling Number One Ibis Colony.

By comparison with the ibis, the giant panda is not nearly so rare. There are still about 1,000 of these large black and white, high-altitude living, bamboo-munching 'cat-bears'. Most of them are in the neighbouring province of Sichuan; a few unlucky, if pampered, ones play star roles in world zoos. In Shaanxi Province there is one special nature reserve for them in Foping County, southwest of Xi'an and not far from the Qinling Ibis Colony.

The orange snub-nosed monkey, also known as the golden-haired monkey, is another inhabitant of the Qinling Mountains. Found in birch forests and mountain gullies, at around 2,500–3,000 metres (8,000–10,000 feet), these very agile, acrobatic animals have bright yellow-orange fur, with white chests, long tails and distinctive blue circles around their eyes.

The so-called Reeves pheasant is the original proud possessor of the long, waving tail feathers worn by generals in Chinese opera. The tail of the male reaches to 100–140 centimetres (3.5–4.5 feet) in length. The bird is found in mountain forests, between 600–2,000 metres (2,000–6,500 feet) above sea level.

The **Xi'an Zoo** in Jinhua Bei Lu (tel 331972) has examples of both giant and lesser pandas, pheasants and orange snub-nosed monkeys as well as northeast China tigers, leopards, Sichuan parrots, wild donkeys and other animals indigenous to China. There are also a number of animals presented to the Xi'an Zoo by the Japanese cities of Kyoto and Nara, with which Xi'an has a formal as well as a historical relationship. The zoo was established in Revolution Park in 1956, but moved to a much larger site to the east in 1976.

Until surveys are published of the complete fauna of southern Shaanxi there will not be a definitive inventory of species. The British traveller, Violet Cressy-Marcks, who interviewed Mao Zedong in Yan'an, recorded in 1938 that in an area 20 miles from the city she saw 'common jay, Chinese jay, blue magpie, golden eagle, pheasants, green woodpeckers, flocks of bustard, wild horned sheep and wild ducks and I was told there were leopards but I did not see any'. Near Xi'an 'there were many sulphur bellied rats, wood and field mice, also mallard, teal, wrens, redstarts, minks and goral'. At Lintong she saw 'geese, ducks, hares, snipe, bustard and mallard'. The wildlife of the Wei River plain is almost certainly much depleted now, in contrast to that of the mountains of the south.

Places of Interest in the Xi'an Area

Period One: Pre-Qin

Background

Xi'an lies a few miles south of the Wei River, a western tributary of the Yellow River. Near the modern city is the ancient site of Chang'an (Everlasting Peace), which served as the capital of several ruling dynasties spanning a period of over 1,000 years. But the Wei valley had been settled much earlier. In fact, both the Wei valley and Shaanxi Province are traditionally known as the 'cradle' of Chinese civilization. The Yellow Emperor—the mythical ancestor and first sovereign of the Han race who is said to have lived in the third millennium BC—has his legendary burial place at Huangling, a town halfway between Xi'an and Yan'an in northern Shaanxi.

PALAEOLITHIC

Before the present landscape of the Wei valley was created from deposits of sand blown from the Mongolian Plateau, man's early ancestors lived in the area. During 1963–66 a skull (now in Beijing), jaw and various other bones of Lantian Man, a form of *Homo erectus* dating to around 800,000 BC, were discovered 38 kilometres (27 miles) southwest of Xi'an.

In the spring of 1978 another startling discovery was made in Dali County, near the provincial border with Shaanxi: an almost complete skull of what is now known as Dali Man. He is thought to belong to an early subspecies of *Homo sapiens*, living in perhaps 300,000 or 200,000 BC.

NEOLITHIC

The development of agriculture found an ideal setting in the Wei and middle Yellow River valleys, with their deep loess deposits containing all the necessary minerals for successful cultivation. From approximately 5000 BC onwards settlements were formed, larger and more permanent than similar ones elsewhere in the world. The early Neolithic stage in China is called Yangshao Culture. The name Painted Pottery Culture is sometimes preferred, which contrasts with the Black Pottery, or Longshan, Culture which followed it. Yangshao Culture lasted until 3000 BC. A typical Yangshao or Painted Pottery Culture settlement has been excavated at Banpo, on the outskirts of Xi'an.

Sights

BANPO MUSEUM

In 1953 when workers were laying the foundations for a factory at Banpo, less than seven kilometres (five miles) east of Xi'an, they came upon the remains of an ancient settlement. The discovery of this New Stone Age village has been described as the 'greatest single contribution to prehistoric archaeology in east Asia' (John Hay, *Ancient China*). Dating from approximately 5000 to 4000 BC, it is the most complete example of an agricultural Neolithic settlement anywhere in the world. Its remarkably well-preserved condition makes it a major attraction for visitors to Xi'an.

Banpo pottery decoration

An area of 4,000 square metres (one acre) has been fully excavated, enclosed and put on view to the public. Foundations of 45 houses have been uncovered, some round, some square. The largest dwelling may have been a communal meeting place, or alternatively the house of the chief. Among the other impressive finds are: 200 storage pots, a collection of pottery and tools, a pottery-making centre and a graveyard with more than 250 graves.

The museum is simply but sensibly laid out. The main hall, in the rear, was built over the excavation site. Two smaller exhibition halls by the entrance display unearthed items, drawings and explanatory notes in both Chinese and English.

From the implements and utensils discovered, archaeologists have learned a great deal about the daily life of Banpo. It was a typical Yangshao Culture community. Two to three hundred people lived there, practising slash-and-burn agriculture. They depended on millet and pork for their existence. In addition to millet, they planted vegetables such as cabbage and mustard, and hemp which was used to make clothing. They kept pigs, dogs and perhaps chickens and other animals. They also hunted and fished. They fired and painted extraordinarily beautiful clay pots with both abstract and non-abstract designs. The earlier decorations on these vessels portrayed fish with mouths open, fishing-nets and deer on the run—subjects reflecting the main preoccupations of Banpo's inhabitants. Gradually, as the displayed pots show quite clearly, the designs became abstract: the fish motif, for instance, was later replaced by a geometric pattern.

Banpo pottery designs

Chinese archaeologists believed that a primitive communist matriarchal clan lived at Banpo. In the communal burial ground found to the north of the site, men and women were buried separately, usually by themselves, sometimes in multiple single-sex graves. Women were generally interred with a greater number of funeral objects than men. However, it has been pointed out by foreign archaeologists that in most early matriarchal settlements, excavated elsewhere, whole families related through the female line have been found buried together.

The Banpo Museum is located at the eastern end of the city, a convenient stop on the way to or from the Terracotta Warriors. It can be reached by bus number 8 from the Bell Tower, or bus number 11 from the Railway Station. It is open every day 9 am–5.30 pm.

REMAINS OF THE CAPITALS OF THE WESTERN ZHOU

Bronze metallurgy was practised from about the middle of the millennium, contemporary with the emergence of the Shang Dynasty. During this period (1600–1027 BC), the Wei and Jing valleys were dominated by a relatively backward people called the Zhou. Under their leader, King Wu, they attacked and captured Anyang, the capital of the Shang in 1027 BC. The Zhou Dynasty lasted formally until 29 BC, but the kings only enjoyed real power until 771 BC. This period is called the Western Zhou. Archaeologists have discovered the remains of two Zhou palaces west of Xi'an, at Fengchu Village, Qishan County, and at Zhaochen Village, Fufeng County.

A **Western Zhou chariot burial pit** was unearthed at **Zhangjiapo**, Chang'an County, in 1955. The war chariot was the pre-eminent symbol of power during the Bronze Age. One of the pits excavated at Zhangjiapo contained two chariots and the remains of six horses and one slave, interred as part of the funeral of a lord. These are on display in a small museum west of the city, near Dou Men village, which is accessible by taxi.

Weaving a Spell

Here was a kaleidoscope of colour beyond belief within a dusty desert place, as refreshingly different as discovering Van Gogh's 'Sunflowers' amongst the murky Manchester factories and figures of Lowry. A sword is brandished above a trailing satin sleeve, the fiery orange of dancing flames. Yellow silk of Sun and Earth is the Emperor's colour, embroidered with a red-tongued golden dragon. Mood is swiftly changed as these vivid silken robes shimmer in the hot caressing breeze, suddenly enlivened by the dramatic overtures of a white-bearded man toward a timid young maiden, as he rushed shrieking to left, to right. The musicians, accommodated at the side of the cast-concrete stage, produce a mixture of melody and sound-effects to fit the action, emotion and body language. The conflict of a sword fight is created by a rapid and voluminous thrashing of drum and cymbal; remorse and contemplation by the sad drone of the two-stringed erhu; gaiety by the bird-like chatter of the dizi bamboo flute; and tranquillity by the subtle plucking of the moon guitar. Exits are made to a flurried finale of everything that the orchestra can muster.

Backstage is the open-air dressing, make-up and green room rolled into one. The trunks of this travelling troupe lay open, overflowing with the finest embroidered silks. Masks, beards, bald heads and head-dresses lie strewn in apparent confusion. Oblivious to the crowd of peasants a young girl makes up as the Empress. She picks up colour from a tiny paint-box, guiding herself with the use of a palm-sized mirror. She pales her oriental complexion to eggshell smoothness. Her slender tapering eyes are accentuated. She pouts her lips to paint on their apex a slim scarlet rosebud, and rouges her cheeks to the subtle tint of a ripening apple. Only then does this girl allow her face to be dimpled by a smile of majestic beauty. Crowned with a head-dress of red silk and silver she enters the stage, followed by ladies of the court to a deafening fanfare.

William Lindesay, Alone on the Great Wall

Western Zhou-dynasty bronze incense burner

It is recorded that the Zhou established five different capitals in the Wei and Jing valleys at different times. Two of these have been identified. **Fengjing** on the eastern bank of the Feng River was an early capital. **Haojing** on the opposite bank was the capital from 1027 to 771 BC. The sites have been excavated and the remains of houses, workshops, burials and some hoards of bronze articles have been found and removed to the Xianyang and Shaanxi History museums. Nothing of the old capitals can now be seen at the original sites.

Period Two: The Qin Empire

Background

THE RISE OF QIN

The Eastern Zhou began with the re-establishment of the capital near Luoyang, Henan Province, in 770 BC. The dynasty is divided into two periods, the Spring and Autumn Annals (770–476 BC) and the Warring States (475–221 BC), both taken from the names of books. During the former the Zhou kings were only nominal leaders and the Chinese world was divided into more than 100 petty principalities; by the beginning of the latter, these had been absorbed into seven much larger states.

The Warring States period saw the beginning of the Iron Age in China, a time of tremendous technological progress in the arts of both war and peace. In due course Qin (Ch'in)—based near modern Xi'an—became the most powerful of the contending states, and flourished as the result of a single-minded emphasis on military prowess, public works and food production.

THE FIRST EMPEROR

In 246 BC King Zheng came to the Qin throne, a mere boy of 13. During his reign Qin superiority was finally established when the six other states were annexed between 230 and 221 BC, unifying China for the first time ever.

Bronze chariot, Qin Terracotta Army Museum

THE FIRST EMPEROR OF CHINA

Qin Shihuangdi, the First Emperor of China, was both a reformer and a tyrant. Although his reign lasted little more than a decade, it was epoch-making in terms of its enduring influence on Chinese civilization.

While the emperor is best known by most people for his amazing tomb with its terracotta guards, perhaps his most valuable legacy is a uniform Chinese script which permits people speaking different regional dialects to have a means of communication. Qin Shihuangdi standardized more than the writing of characters, however. The demands of trade required a currency with a recognized fixed value throughout his vast conquered territory, so he standardized the coinage, introducing a circular copper coin with a square hole in the centre. Equally important reforms were the standardization of weights and measures, and codification of the law.

To organize the empire Qin Shihuangdi abolished the prevailing feudal system and established prefectures and counties. These were put under the administration of officials appointed by the central government. Such extensive control required roads, which Qin Shihuangdi ordered to be built, the main ones radiating from his capital, Xianyang. To protect his northern border against hostile nomads, he strengthened the pre-existing fortifications, and the line of defence now known as the Great Wall is attributed to him. It is said that he joined up stretches of frontier walls that were constructed by his predecessors to make one long barrier.

Chinese tour guides and literature promote the Great Wall as a symbol of China's ancient civilization, but in the eyes of modern Chinese it epitomizes their country's isolation and backwardness. Its construction was achieved at huge expense, particularly in terms of human lives. Labourers were conscripted to work on the wall, and convicts served out sentences there. Some convict labourers even had 'perpetual' sentences, which meant that when they died their places were inherited by family members.

There are many folk tales recounting the horrors of forced labour. The legend of Meng Jiangnu is the best known. Meng Jiangnu's husband had been conscripted to work for a season on the Great Wall. When, by the end of summer, he had still not returned to his Shaanxi home, she decided to take him warm clothes for the winter. After a difficult journey she found his work gang in Hebei, but his fellow conscripts told Meng that her husband had already died. At this tragic news, Meng began to cry hysterically, and her flood of tears broke open a part of the Great Wall, revealing her husband's remains. He had been buried where he fell and his body was used as part of the fill for the wall.

On hearing of the damage to his project, an enraged Qin Shihuangdi, coincidentally present on an inspection tour, ordered Meng to be brought before him. His fury soon subsided on seeing her beauty. Although he offered to take her as concubine, she decided that death was preferable and threw herself into the Yellow Sea.

The emperor did not live long and his death in 210 BC, while away from his capital on tour, led to the fall of his dynasty shortly after. There is a story of how his Prime Minister, fearful that news of the emperor's death would spark rebellion, tried to conceal it. The emperor's body was transported in haste back to Xianyang, the Qin capital near modern Xi'an. To mask the stench of the putrefying corpse, the minister filled his chariot with rotting fish. But the feared revolt was only postponed; four years later Qin Shihuangdi's heir was killed by rebels and the Han Dynasty was established soon after.

Characters of 'An' (peace), and 'Ma' (horse), used by the Six Warring States (annexed by the Kingdom of Qin)

Qi	Chu	Yan	Han	Zhao	Wei
齐	楚	燕	韩	赵	魏

秦 *Common characters, Qin Dynasty*

Ma (horse)

An (peace)

Drawn by Wang Fan

(following pages) Qin terracotta troops in Pit Number One

King Zheng took the title of Qin Shihuangdi, First Emperor of Qin. (The term *huangdi* had previously only been used for deities and mythological hero-rulers such as the Yellow Emperor. Qin itself is the origin of our word 'China'.) His capital was at Xianyang (see page 56), northwest of the present-day town, on the north bank of the Wei River.

An emperor of vast ambitions and achievements, Qin Shihuangdi had a profound influence on Chinese history and culture, both in his life and death. The colossal scale and careful detail of his army of terracotta warriors (see below) shows beyond any doubt the advanced state of artistic and technological development of ancient Chinese culture, which historians in China have always claimed.

The great clay army is certainly also a fitting memorial to the man who first really united what were until then disparate states. Qin Shihuangdi, who has been called both tyrant and reformer, ruled over a vast territory. Having gained predominance over various ruling houses, he became the sole source of power and final authority for a centralized government in Xianyang. To consolidate his huge empire, he introduced several important reforms: he personally supervised the organization of a uniform Chinese written language and prescribed 100 officially approved surnames for all his subjects.

The First Emperor's government was severe. He administered a strict legal code, whereby a whole family would be executed for the crimes of one of its members; he taxed people and conscripted millions of labourers for both military and civil projects. To safeguard the northern frontier, the existing defensive lines along the border were rebuilt and extended to become China's Great Wall. Armies were sent as far south as today's Vietnam. Roads, irrigation schemes, palaces and above all his mausoleum all required hordes of reluctant labourers. Out of a total population of 20 million, one and a half million are thought to have been called to some form of service to the State. At the same time, independent thought was suppressed: books whose contents were considered subversive were burned, and hundreds of scholars buried alive. These oppressive policies caused suffering on a huge scale, and on Qin Shihuangdi's death revolts swiftly followed.

Sights

QIN TERRACOTTA ARMY MUSEUM
One of the major sites of interest in China, this is an archaeological find on a monumental scale. Literally an army of sculptured warriors—no two exactly alike—it is a stunning display that every visitor to China should see.

The discovery of the terracotta soldiers was like a legend come true for the villagers living in the area. For centuries they had been telling stories about the ghosts who lived underground and who were unearthed whenever they dug. Then, during a drought in the spring of 1974, some farmers decided to sink a well at a spot less than one and a half kilometres (less than a mile) east of the First Emperor's Mausoleum. This happened to be exactly at right angles to the centre of the original outer enclosure. As the farmers dug, they came upon (in the words of *Newsweek*), 'the clay clones of an 8,000-man army'.

When the first figures were unearthed, it was not appreciated how many there were, but gradually the significance of the discovery was realized: the emperor had decided to take an army with him to the nether world.

Whether he meant actually to move the whole army nearer to his own tomb, or to make this location the warriors' permanent resting place, is still unknown. Some archaeologists think this could have been merely a storage place for his figures. But excavations are still being carried out, albeit at a painstakingly slow pace, and new discoveries may continue to be unearthed for many years to come.

The Qin Terracotta Army Museum, which opened in 1979, is a large hangar-like building constructed over Pit Number One, the place of the original discovery in 1974. There are two exhibition halls outside the main building, in which are displayed bronze chariots (see below) and an assortment of pottery figures and horses (touched up in what are believed to be the original colours) and weapons.

The terracotta figures were found in a vault five metres (16 feet) below the surface. The vault was originally built with walls of pounded earth, and a wooden roof was added before the enclosure was sealed. It appears that the troops of General Xiang Yu, who had already plundered the nearby imperial tomb, Qin Ling, opened the vault in 206 BC and set fire to the roof, which collapsed, smashing the terracottas *in situ* and preserving them in mud and ash.

■ TERRACOTTA TROOPS

The terracotta soldiers are remarkably realistic pieces of sculpture. Each soldier's face has individual features, prompting speculation that they were modelled from life. They have squarish faces with broad foreheads and large, thick-lipped mouths, and they wear neat moustaches, and a number have beards. Some of them have their hair in a topknot. Expressions are generally austere, eyes focused far ahead. The figures are mostly 1.8 metres (5 feet 11 inches) in height. The lower part of the body is solid, the upper part hollow. They were originally painted, but the colour has been almost entirely lost.

The soldiers are divided into infantry armed with swords and spears, archers, crossbow archers, cavalry, chariot drivers and officers. The chariots no longer exist

except for their metal fittings. They were almost certainly real ones, made of wood. Each is drawn by four pottery horses, on average 1.5 metres (4 feet 11 inches) tall by 2 metres (6 feet 7 inches) long.

The terracotta troops bear real arms, made of bronze. A huge number have been unearthed: swords, daggers, billhooks, spears, halberds, axes, crossbow triggers, and arrowheads. The copper-tin alloy used was combined with 11 other elements such as nickel, magnesium, cobalt and chrome, and many weapons have emerged sharp, shiny and untarnished. The arrow-heads contain a poisonous percentage of lead.

■ THE EXCAVATIONS
Pit Number One
This pit, the first of three that were discovered over the period May 1974 to June 1976, forms the main exhibition hall at the Qin Terracotta Army Museum complex.

It consists of 11 parallel corridors running east to west, each corridor being 210 metres (230 yards) in length. The vault covers a total area of 12,600 square metres (14,350 square yards). A section of 960 square metres (1,148 square yards) has been fully excavated and marked out as the centrepiece of the museum. So far, more than 2,000 warriors have been unearthed, but investigations suggest that up to 6,000 more lie beneath the dusty substrate in this vault alone.

The excavated soldiers face east in battle formation. Three rows, each of 70 lightly armed archers, form the vanguard. They are followed by 38 columns of more heavily armoured infantry interspersed with war chariots, of which only the pottery horses remain. A single column of spearmen face north, south and west.

Visitors enter the vault through the east door and walk towards the south, past a red carpeted staircase (usually covered in plastic sheeting) reserved for visiting VIPs. At the foot of this staircase, the very spot of the original discovery back in the drought-stricken spring of 1974 is marked. Proceeding down the southern flank of the vault you cross the excavations on an elevated walkway which affords views of both the completely excavated area looking back east and the partially excavated area to the western end of the vault. Now continuing down the northern flank of the vault you see corridors covered in protective plastic, and may occasionally catch a glimpse of a terracotta warrior half excavated, looking as if he was drowning in a sea of yellow mud. Visitors can exit the vault from a small door in the very northwest corner and move on to inspect Pit Number Three.

Pit Number Two
Discovered just one month after Pit Number Two (see below), Pit Number Three lies 25 metres (82 feet) to the northwest of Pit Number One. At only 28.8 metres (94.5 feet) in length from east to west, 24.6 metres in width from north to south and cover-

Archer, Qin Terracotta Army

ing an area of 500 square metres (598 square feet), Pit Number Three is by far the smallest of the three vaults. Nevertheless, archaeologists believe that, containing as it does a war chariot, 68 warriors and numerous bronze weapons, Pit Number Three represents the headquarters of the garrison guarding Qin Shihuangdi in the afterlife, exercising military control over the other two larger pits of infantry.

Pit Number Three is housed within a modern building. The excavations are well labelled and atmospherically illuminated by spotlights rather than by natural light as in Pit Number One. Bilingual interpretive panels are positioned on the surrounding hand rails, and colour photographs give the visitor a useful retrospective of the excavation process, at the same time conveying something of the excitement at unearthing such a treasure trove.

The excavations lie between 5.2 and 5.4 metres (17 and 17.7 feet) below ground. Terracotta warriors, mainly headless, and the four draught horses of a chariot stand upon a fine Qin brick floor. Within the pit, rammed earth walls form chambers housing small detachments. Timbers once completed this subterranean vault structure, but these had collapsed and caused irreparable damage to the warriors beneath. Although many of the figures are decapitated, they compensate for their damage by exhibiting fine pigmentation.

Pit Number Two

(This pit is not yet open to the public.) Called Pit Number Two, the L-shaped vault was found northeast of Pit Number One in May 1976. Preliminary examination of the site suggested that a cache of perhaps 1,000 terracotta warriors lay in wait. The Pit was filled in and over a decade later, in 1988, investigation recommenced. Excavations were still proceeding in late 1992. Archaeologists say that some 6,000 pottery figurines will eventually be displayed. A building to convert Pit Number Two into an *in situ* museum is simultaneously under construction while the excavations continue.

■ THE BRONZE CHARIOTS

Housed in the exhibition hall to the left-hand side of the hangar built over the terracotta warriors are two magnificent bronze chariots.

In August 1978 archaeologists recovered a gold ornament the size of a walnut as they took samples around the mausoleum of the First Emperor. Two years later the chariots were recovered and in the following year, 1981, the discovery was announced. Black and white pictures illustrating the progressive excavation are posted on the walls of the exhibition room.

The larger of the two chariots weighs 1,200 kilograms (2,646 pounds) and at 2.86 metres (9.38 feet) in length and 1.07 metres (3.51 feet) in height is thought to be half

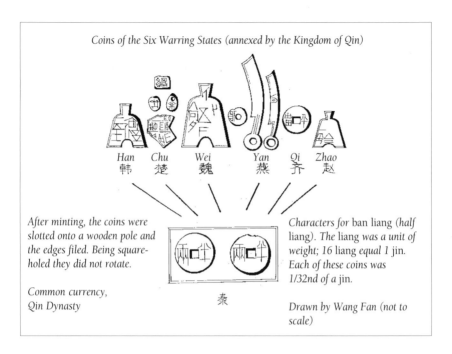

Coins of the Six Warring States (annexed by the Kingdom of Qin)

Han   Chu   Wei   Yan   Qi   Zhao
韩   楚   魏   燕   齐   赵

After minting, the coins were slotted onto a wooden pole and the edges filed. Being square-holed they did not rotate.

Common currency, Qin Dynasty

Characters for ban liang (half liang). The liang was a unit of weight; 16 liang equal 1 jin. Each of these coins was 1/32nd of a jin.

秦

Drawn by Wang Fan (not to scale)

the actual size. The chariot therefore seems likely to have been crafted specifically for Qin Shihuangdi's afterlife, although it is thought he used such a vehicle for his inspection tours. Called *anche* (safe chariot), this was the limousine of its day. Rhombus-shaped lattice windows are set into all four sides of the carriage for ventilation. The roof is an umbrella-like canopy which also extends over the driver to provide shade. Stylized clouds are painted on the interior ceiling and, from silk fragments discovered inside, it is thought some accessories—maybe cushions or quilts—had once made the royal passenger comfortable. This predates the more widespread use and export of silk by several centuries.

The second chariot on display may have been a vanguard chariot, running before that of the emperor. It is also drawn by four horses. Horsepower to weight ratio suggests that both these vehicles could have covered ground fairly swiftly. There is no compartment in the vanguard chariot; to accommodate the standing driver the canopy is correspondingly much higher than that of the *anche*.

Both chariots highlight the superb metallurgical and metal-shaping technology of the Qin period, as well as its highest artistic standards. Most fittings are of solid bronze, often painted, although their pigments have faded. The harness and reins are inlaid with gold and silver, and each horse wears a halter made of some 84 one-

The Long Longing

Endless is my longing—longing for Chang'an.
When autumn crickets hum by the gold edge of the well,
A light frost casts cold colours on my mat,
The solitary lamp is dim; my longing near despair.
I furl the curtain and look upon the moon,
In vain, I sigh . . . .
Like a flower is my fair one, sever'd by cloud and mist.
Above, the faint blue sky,
Beneath, the green water wave . . . .
High is heaven, wide is earth;
Neither can my spirit fly,
Nor my dreams carry me over the grim mountain pass.
Long is the longing that crushes my heart!

Li Bo (699–762), translated by Moon Kwan

長相思　李白

長相思
在長安
絡緯秋啼金井闌
微霜淒淒簟色寒
孤燈不明思欲絕
卷帷望月空長嘆
美人如花隔雲端
上有青冥之高天
下有淥水之波瀾
天長路遠魂飛苦
夢魂不到關山難
長相思
摧心肝

centimetre (0.4-inch)-long tubes, fitted one onto another and thus endowed with a flexibility close to rope or leather. The canopies are incredibly thin bronze sheets but their casting is even and smooth. They are laid over a frame of 36 bow-shaped spokes about six millimetres (0.24 inch) in diameter. All these dimensions suggest to the archaeologists that both the temperature control and the casting methods were by this time highly advanced. In total the emperor's chariot has 3,462 separate components of gold, silver or bronze.

The chariot drivers and horses are also of solid bronze, yet despite their material they appear lifelike. Artisans probably used files on the figures to reproduce the appearance of hair. The horses, painted white to mimic hide and given realistically flared nostrils, convey the impression that they are ready to stride forth at the crack of the charioteer's whip.

Models of the chariots can be purchased at most tourist outlets in the city. They range in price from a few *yuan* for plastic copies to several thousands of *yuan* for bronze designs.

QIN LING, THE MAUSOLEUM OF THE FIRST EMPEROR

Qin Shihuangdi began supervising the construction of the Qin Ling, his burial tomb, as soon as he took the throne in 246 BC. Work intensified after the conquest of the rival states, with 700,000 labourers conscripted to build it. The site chosen was south of the Wei River beside the slopes of Black Horse Mountain in what is now Lintong County, 30 kilometres (18 miles) from Xi'an. The exterior of the mausoleum is in the form of a low earth pyramid with a wide base. Preliminary investigation by the Chinese has confirmed that there was an inner and outer enclosure. The mausoleum is thought to have been plundered at least once, by a rebel general called Xiang Yu (Hsiang Yu) in 206 BC, but no excavations have yet been done. Chinese archaeologists are reluctant to open the tomb until they know a way to preserve what may be very delicate remains.

It is known, however, that not only was the body of Qin Shihuangdi interred in the tomb (in 209 BC, a year after his death), but also those of his childless wives—who were buried alive—together with artisans who had knowledge of the inner structure of the mausoleum.

Information about the construction of the mausoleum comes almost entirely from the brush of Sima Qian (Ssu-ma Ch'ien), the author of *The Historical Records*, China's first large-scale work of history which was written about a century after the fall of Qin.

According to Sima, heaven and earth were represented in the central chamber of the tomb. The ceiling formed the sky with pearls for stars. The floor was of a physical map of the world in stone; the 100 rivers of the empire flowed mechanically with mercury. All manner of treasures were piled inside for the emperor's opulent afterlife. Crossbows were set up and positioned to shoot automatically if the interior was disturbed. After it was sealed the tomb was grassed over to appear as a natural hill. It is still like that today, although a stairway has now been built to the top, from which there is a good view of the surrounding area.

Near the mausoleum many ancillary tombs have been discovered. Some occupants were probably victims of the Second Emperor in the power struggle following the death of Qin Shihuangdi. In addition, some large graves, suspected to be those of Qin Shihuangdi's parents, have also been discovered in the area, as well as the graves of a general and of some 70 Qin labourers together with large numbers of horse skeletons. None of the sites of these finds have so far been put on view to the public.

REMAINS OF XIANYANG

Xianyang, a satellite city of Xi'an, was established on the north bank of the Wei River in around 350 BC, when Qin was one of several warring states vying for supremacy. The city was adopted as the Qin capital, and is said to have developed into a metropolis with 800,000 inhabitants before rebel general Xiang Yu set fire to it in 206 BC.

In 1961 the exact location of the city was re-discovered in the Yaodian People's Commune northwest of Xi'an. Excavations in the 1960s and 1970s revealed the foundations of the **Xianyang Palace**, the First Emperor's principal domicile, partly built on a terrace of pounded earth. The structure and function of different parts of the palace are now known. Important discoveries were made, including the remains of some murals. Building materials, decorated bricks and tiles were found in large quantities. These remains, and a model of the palace, can be seen in the **Xianyang Museum**. Most visitors, however, go to the museum to view its collection of miniature terracotta soldiers dating from the Han Dynasty (see page 63).

Now Xianyang is Shaanxi's booming third city, site of the new airport serving Xi'an, 28 kilometres (17 miles away).

REMAINS OF AFANG PALACE

In 212 BC the First Emperor decided to build a new and larger principal palace on the other side of the Wei River, some 10 kilometres (6 miles) west of Xi'an. Afang Palace was never finished, but the raised platform of pounded earth remains to this day.

Period Three: The Han Dynasty

Background

The Qin Dynasty maintained its authority only until 209 BC. The First Emperor's death in 210 BC was followed by outbreaks of rebellion and civil war, which led to the empire's dissolution. The final blow was dealt by General Xiang Yu, who conquered the Qin forces in 207 BC. But then he himself was overthrown four years later by the founder of the Han Dynasty.

The first Han emperor was a general of plebeian background called Liu Bang (Liu Pang), known posthumously by his dynastic title of Han Gaozu (Han Kao-tsu), which literally means Great-great-grandfather of Han. His capital, called Chang'an, was built in the strategic Wei valley. Accordingly the first half of Han rule, lasting until AD 8, is called the Western Han to distinguish it from the Eastern Han period, AD 25–220, when the capital was at Luoyang.

THE CAPITAL CITY OF CHANG'AN

In 202 BC Liu Bang moved into a minor Qin palace on the southern side of the Wei. Later the architect Xiao He added a large new complex of some 40 buildings to the west of it. This was the **Weiyang Palace** (see page 63), which was to remain the principal seat of the Western Han emperors. Together these two palaces formed the nucleus of Han-dynasty Chang'an.

The imperial establishment soon outgrew the two original palaces and more buildings were added during the time of the Emperor Han Huidi (reigned 194–187 BC). An irregular-shaped wall was built around the palaces, eventually forming a circumference of about 22 kilometres (14 miles). Within the wall there were eight main streets and 160 alleys. Outside the wall another city developed, a city of artisans, with markets, workshops and houses.

THE SILK ROAD

It was during the Han that central and western Asia was opened up to the Chinese. This was to have a profound impact on Chang'an.

From the capital, Han Wudi (Han Wu-ti), the Martial Emperor (reigned 140–86 BC), launched a series of campaigns against the Xiongnu, the warlike Turkish people of the steppes, who were a constant threat to the northern frontier of China. In 139 BC Zhang Qian (Chang Ch'ien) was sent officially to central Asia to find allies against the Xiongnu. On his second journey in 119 BC he went as far as the Ili Valley, on the present-day border with the CIS, and from there despatched envoys to India and the

THE PEASANT PAINTERS OF HUXIAN

In 1958, a group of farmers in Huxian, a county some 40 kilometres (25 miles) outside Xi'an, did some paintings to record progress on the construction of a new reservoir. So successful were the works that they inspired the organization of special painting centres to help the peasants develop their art. By the mid-1970s, there were about 2,000 active painters in the county, all of them farmers who would bicycle to the centres after a hard day's work in the fields. These centres are still the support system of Huxian's peasant artists. Painting materials and a certain amount of professional guidance are given, but the basic technical tuition does not seem to have squashed the creative independence of the better painters of the Huxian group.

The distinctive style developed by the Huxian painters has won them national, and international, recognition. Exhibitions have already been held in Hong Kong, Sweden, London, the US and Canada, as well as in Beijing and Shanghai.

The paintings are a complete contrast from the misty landscapes and muted colours of classic Chinese watercolours. The work of the peasants of Huxian is humorous, vibrant, dependent on brilliant colour and intricate surface pattern, sometimes with a total disregard for perspective. A hint of the intricate design of local embroidery is carried through to the paintings.

Themes chosen reflect the painters' everyday life as farmers—drying fish, feeding chicks, reeling silk, wedding parties and other festivities. Some painters record, with an almost childlike accuracy of observation, change within their society—horses hauling carts of concrete, for example, or a confrontation between an ox-drawn cart and a tractor. Legend and traditional opera stories are also a rich source of themes for the painters.

The group claims that over 100,000 paintings have already been produced. Some 200 paintings are on display in eight rooms at the modest Huxian Peasant Painting Exhibition Hall, about a one-and-a-half-hour taxi-ride from Xi'an.

Visitors to Xi'an will find a small selection of paintings on sale at the Jianguo Hotel Friendship Shopping Mall. But top quality work from the most creative artists of the group is more difficult to come by, and much more expensive. The work of Wang Jinglong, which is strikingly different from most of the group, has already aroused worldwide interest on account of its distinctive individual interpretation of everyday happenings. Luo Zhijin and Liu Fengtao are two other names to look for.

The pictures on this page
are reproduced courtesy of
the Alvin Gallery, Hong
Kong, which has been
responsible of exhibiting
some of the best work of the
Huxian painters.

*Family Plots in the Countryside (above); Pulling Concrete (below);
Huxian paintings by Wang Jinglong*

Iranian Empire as well as kingdoms east of the Caspian Sea. One of the most influential finds that Zhang Qian made on this journey were the splendid horses in what is now Uzbekistan. Some of these were brought to China where they later became the inspiration of Chinese sculptors, painters and writers to an extent that was almost obsessional, especially during the Tang Dynasty.

Merchant caravans followed the armies and established the routes of what Europeans later called the Silk Road. The eastern section opened by the Chinese linked up with trade routes in western Asia to form lines of trade and cultural exchange stretching from Chang'an to the Mediterranean. Official contact with the Roman Empire was attempted in AD 97, but the envoy never got through. However, unofficial representatives of Rome, including a party of jugglers in AD 120, did arrive in Chang'an. There was a special street where foreigners were accommodated, and even a protocol department to arrange the formal side of their reception.

Paper was one of many Chinese inventions that eventually reached Europe via the Silk Road. The world's earliest pieces of paper were discovered in 1957 at Ba Bridge, east of Xi'an. It was originally thought that paper was invented during the Eastern Han, but these pieces of hemp paper were made considerably earlier, during the reign of Han Wudi.

THE IMPERIAL TOMBS OF THE WESTERN HAN DYNASTY
There are nine tombs of the Western Han emperors on the north bank of the Wei and two south of the present city of Xi'an. The construction of each one was started soon after the accession of the sovereign and, according to regulations, one third of all State revenues was devoted to the project. On the death of the emperor valuable objects were placed in the tomb and the body was interred in a suit of jade plates, sewn together with gold wire. A piece of jade was placed in the mouth of the emperor. Prominent members of the imperial family and important officials were buried in smaller ancillary or satellite tombs nearby.

None of the imperial mausoleums has been excavated, and they remain irregular flat-topped grassy pyramids, 33–46 metres (110–150 feet) above the plain.

Sights

MAO LING, THE MAUSOLEUM OF EMPEROR HAN WUDI
Mao Ling is the tomb of Han Wudi, the Martial Emperor, who came to the throne in 140 BC, ruling for 54 years. Like Qin Shihuangdi, he initiated a new period of dynamic expansion. Imperial rule was extended to the southeast coastal region of China, northern Vietnam and northern Korea. His tomb is 40 kilometres (25 miles) west of Xi'an. Although it has not been excavated, the commemorative area has been

well laid out. The top of the small hill on which a monument has been built has a good view of many surrounding tombs, some of which have been excavated.

The Martial Emperor had tried to avoid his burial with attempts at making himself immortal. He put a bronze statue (the Brazen Immortal) in a high tower to catch the pure dew in a bowl, which he drank with powdered jade. However, the potion proved ineffective, and he died in his 70th year. Apparently there were so many treasures intended for his tomb that they could not all be fitted in. But many of his books are said to have been buried with him, as well as a number of live animals.

The mausoleum was desecrated, rather than robbed, by peasant rebels called the Red Eyebrows, just before the establishment of the Eastern Han. They removed articles from the tomb and threw them on a bonfire. Archaeologists believe that they have found the patch of burnt earth where this happened.

Mao Ling is situated northwest of Xi'an, a convenient stop on the way to or from Qian Ling, the Tang-dynasty tombs (see page 73).

THE TOMB OF HUO QUBING

About one and a half kilometres (under a mile) from the mausoleum of the Martial Emperor is the even more interesting tomb of his eminent general, nicknamed the 'Swift Cavalry General'. Huo Qubing, later Grand Marshal, was born in 140 BC. His uncle took him to fight the fierce northern nomads, the Xiongnu, when he was 18. He died at the age of only 24. According to the author Sima Qian, who was a contemporary, the Martial Emperor built a special tomb for the general in the shape of the Qilian Mountain (which marks the present-day border of Gansu and Qinghai provinces), where Huo had won a great victory.

The tomb has been almost certainly identified by the discovery of 16 remarkable stone sculptures. All are at the site. They are of horses (one of them apparently trampling a Xiongnu), various animals including a tiger, boar, elephant and ox, and two strange human figures, perhaps demons or gods, one of which is wrestling with a bear. This last stone, about 2.77 metres (nine feet) high, may represent a Xiongnu idol. Huo Qubing brought back at least one of these, known as the 'Golden Man'.

On top of the steep-sided tomb mound is a derelict temple. This dates to the last dynasty and has no connection with the tomb.

Beside the two galleries where the stone sculptures are displayed is a **museum**. The exhibits are almost all of the Western Han period and were discovered in the area of the Mao Ling.

There are a number of bronze articles, including money, agricultural implements and a magnificent rhinoceros, though the latter is now in the Shaanxi Museum and only a reproduction is on display. There are also examples of the decorated building materials for which both the Qin and Han were famous.

Han-dynasty earthen tomb figurine

Remains of the Han City of Chang'an

■ HAN CITY WALLS

The site of the Han capital is on the northwestern edge of the present-day city of Xi'an. Today the walls are still there but inside the palaces have been replaced by fields of wheat and rapeseed.

■ REMAINS OF WEIYANG PALACE

The southern part of the Han city was excavated in 1957–9 so the layout of the palaces is known. The raised area of the audience hall of Weiyang Palace, the principal seat of the Western Han emperors, can be reached by road. The platform is 101 metres (330 feet) long, much smaller than was thought for the original hall, but we know that the Weiyang was rebuilt several times during the Tang period, so it is likely that the foundations have been altered.

■ HAN CITY ARMOURY

Built in 200 BC, the armoury occupied 23 hectares (57 acres) near the present-day village of Daliuzhai, next to the site of Weiyang Palace. Excavations have revealed a large number of iron weapons, and some made of bronze. At the end of 1981 it was announced that a number of hefty suits of armour had been found weighing 35–40 kilograms (77–88 pounds).

Han Terracotta Army

The prime exhibit in the Xianyang Museum (see page 56) is a superb collection of 3,000 miniature terracotta warriors from the tomb of Han Gaozu who, as Liu Bang, founded the Han Dynasty in 206 BC. These warriors were found in 1965 in two of a group of Han tombs known as Yangjiawan Tombs.

The terracotta infantryman and cavalrymen, about 35 and 50 centimeters (13.8 and 19.7 inches) in height respectively, are naive in form. Traces of their original colours are barely visible. Like a massive army poised for battle, the warriors are nevertheless an impressive sight that makes the ride from Xi'an well worthwhile.

The museum is on Zhongshan Jie which is a continuation of Xining Jie. Visitors not wanting to hurry back to Xi'an can lodge in either of Xianyang's two hotels open to foreigners—the **Qindu Hotel** on Shengli Jie, Anding Lu or the **Rainbow Guesthouse** on Caihong Lu.

Xianyang is accessible from Xi'an by rail, mini bus or public bus. Mini buses, departing frequently from the bus station near the southwest corner of the city wall, are quite comfortable and cheap (3 *yuan* at the time of writing). The ride takes 30–40 minutes. Alternatively a taxi could be hired for about 120 *yuan*.

Period Four: The Tang Dynasty

Background

The collapse of the Han Dynasty in AD 220 after years of insoluble economic and political problems was followed by centuries of power struggles, barbarian invasions and political fragmentation, with interludes of unity and order. In AD 581 a high ranking official, Yang Qian, seized the throne and founded the Sui Dynasty.

THE SUI AND THE CAPITAL CITY OF DAXINGCHENG

The old Han city of Chang'an was by then too derelict to serve as the symbol of power for the first Sui emperor, who reigned with the title of Wendi (Wen-ti). He commissioned a brilliant engineer, Yuwen Kai, to build a new city—Daxingcheng, or the City of Great Revival—southeast of the old one.

Yang Qian and Yuwen Kai created one of the greatest planned cities, perhaps *the* greatest. The huge rectangular area designated for the metropolis faced the four cardinal points and had an outer wall with a perimeter of over 36 kilometres (22 miles).

The Sui Dynasty was, however, short lived. Wendi was succeeded by his even more ambitious son, the Emperor Sui Yangdi (Sui Yangti). He, in turn, ordered the construction of a new capital at Luoyang, as well as a huge programme of canal building (the Grand Canal, the world's largest man-made waterway running from Luoyang to Hangzhou, was his most monumental legacy to China). He also attempted a disastrous invasion of Korea. Rebellions followed and the emperor was assassinated in Yangzhou in AD 618.

THE ESTABLISHMENT OF THE TANG DYNASTY

Power was next seized by the Li family. Li Yuan, hereditary Duke of Tang, marched on Daxingcheng in AD 617 and the following year made himself emperor with the title of Tang Gaozu (T'ang Kao-tzu). The capital was renamed Chang'an, a deliberate move to assume by implication the mantle of the Han. In turn, Tang Gaozu was ousted by his second son, Li Shimin, who took the throne himself with the title of Tang Taizong (T'ang T'ai-tsung), and effectively consolidated the Tang.

The Tang Dynasty is widely considered to be a Golden Age, the point in history when Chinese civilization reached its most glorious and sophisticated stage. The Tang empire was the largest, richest, most sophisticated state in the world. And Xi'an (Chang'an) was again the centre and symbol of this glory, the world's largest and most splendid city. Only the Baghdad of Harun al Rashid offered any comparison. During this period, Xi'an's city wall stretched far beyond the one standing today,

Tang-dynasty mural at the tomb of Princess Yongtai (reproduction)

which was built during the later Ming period and went as far as the Big Goose Pagoda. By the middle of the eighth century China had a population estimated at 53 million, of which nearly two million lived in the capital.

EMPRESS WU

Taizong died in AD 649 and was succeeded by his ninth son, who reigned with the title of Gaozong until 683. However, the next effective ruler was a woman, not a man. Wu Zetian (see page 82) was born in AD 624 and became a concubine of Taizong. On his death she withdrew from court and became a Buddhist nun, only to be recalled by Gaozong, eventually becoming his empress in AD 655.

After Gaozong's death Wu Zetian dethroned two of her sons and her official reign began in AD 690. Although Empress Wu's rule was characterized by recurrent palace intrigues and ruthless political murders, China prospered greatly during this time.

For economic as well as political reasons she preferred Luoyang to Chang'an and chose this as her capital from AD 683 to 701. Just before her death in AD 705, when she was in her 80s, she was finally removed from power, and the Tang re-established.

THE REIGN OF EMPEROR TANG XUANZONG

The period of struggle over the Tang succession was ended by the emergence of the third great ruler of the dynasty, Emperor Xuanzong, Empress Wu's grandson. Popularly known as Ming Huang, the Enlightened Emperor, his reign corresponds with what is called the High Tang, the apogee of the Tang Dynasty, that most confident and cosmopolitan of all phases of Chinese civilization.

The emperor presided over a brilliant, extravagant court, patronizing the greatest concentration of literary and artistic genius in Chinese history. Xuanzong's contemporaries included the paramount poets of China, Du Fu (AD 712–770), and Li Bai (Li Po, AD 699–762), and the great painter, Wu Daozi (Wu Tao-tzu, AD 700–760).

After the death of his beloved Imperial Concubine (see page 78), Xuanzong died a broken man in AD 762, having earlier abdicated in favour of his third son.

CHANG'AN IN THE EIGHTH CENTURY

Chang'an in the eighth century was a lively, crowded, beautiful city. Appropriately, as the planned capital of a well-ordered society, it was also highly organized.

In the centre was the Imperial City with the Imperial Secretariat, the Imperial Chancellery, the Censorate and the Department of State Affairs under which came the six Boards of Personnel, Revenue, Rites, War, Justice and Public Works. This organization of government lasted, in this form at least, for the next thousand years.

The central north–south avenue, with the delightful name of 'The Street of the Vermilion Bird', divided the Outer City into two districts: the area of the aristocrats

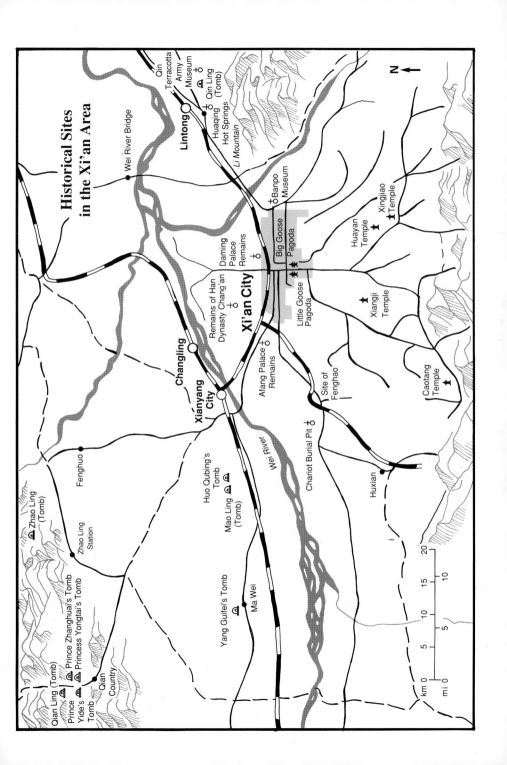

Historical Sites in the Xi'an Area

N

Qin Terracotta Army Museum
Qin Ling (Tomb)
Huaqing Hot Springs
Li Mountain
Wei River Bridge
Lintong

Banpo Museum
Daming Palace Remains
Big Goose Pagoda
Xingjiao Temple
Huayan Temple
Remains of Han Dynasty Chang'an
Xi'an City
Little Goose Pagoda
Xiangji Temple
Changling
Afang Palace Remains
Site of Fenghao
Xianyang City
Caotang Temple
Huo Qubing's Tomb
Mao Ling (Tomb)
Chariot Burial Pit
Fenghuo
Wei River
Huxian
Zhao Ling (Tomb)
Zhao Ling Station
Yang Guifei's Tomb
Ma Wei
Qian Ling (Tomb)
Prince Zhanghuai's Tomb
Prince Yide's Tomb
Princess Yongtai's Tomb
Qian Country

km 0   5   10   15   20
mi 0   5   10

to the east, and the rather more populated section of the merchants and lower classes to the west. The two markets which served them were very large and extremely well run. We know that the shops and workshops of the East Market were divided into 220 trades, each one with its own exclusive area and bazaar.

Much of the colour in Chang'an was provided by the 'Westerners' — merchants from central Asia and Arabia, and particularly travellers from Persia.

Central Asian fashions dominated the capital. Women dressed in the Persian style and wore exotic Western jewellery. Men played polo. The Buddhist temples and monasteries vied with each other in offering unusual religious entertainments.

Foreigners congregated in the West Market, which was always full of excitement and activity. Here were bazaars and artisans' workshops, merchants' houses and hostelries, taverns and entertainment places, including wine shops where the songs and dances of central Asia were performed. There were Persian bazaars; shops of the unpopular Uygar (Uighur) moneylenders; and markets selling precious jewels and pearls, spices, medicinal herbs, silk, and a whole range of everyday items, including the newly fashionable beverage, tea. This was where criminals were punished and where courtesans could be found. Many of these ladies were from the lands bordering Persia and some were reputedly even blond and blue-eyed.

Tang-dynasty gold coffin and silver outer casket

Tri-colour glazed figure, Tang Dynasty

FOREIGN RELIGIONS IN CHANG'AN

For much of the Tang the authorities allowed the foreign communities freedom of religion. Zoroastrianism, Manichaeism, Nestorianism and finally Islam all followed Buddhism to Chang'an (see pages 88–90).

If you are interested in tracing the development of these religions, Xi'an's Shaanxi Museum (see page 110) provides some intriguing evidence. Here you can see a tombstone, dated AD 874, inscribed in Chinese and Persian Pahlavi script, originally marking the grave of Ma, wife of Suren, a Zoroastrian. Also at the museum, in the Forest of Steles, is the celebrated Nestorian Stele. Inscriptions on this stone, in Chinese and Syriac, record the establishment of Chang'an's second Nestorian Christian chapel in 781.

The Manichees, who believed in a combination of Gnostic Christianity and Zoroastrianism, also had a place of worship in Chang'an in the eighth century.

THE INFLUENCE OF CHANG'AN

If Chang'an itself was cosmopolitan, it also had unparalleled influence throughout central and eastern Asia. The royal progeny of several Korean and central Asian states, as well as Tibet, were educated in the schools and monasteries of the Tang capital. But by far the greatest transfer of Tang culture was to Japan. From the mid-seventh century to the end of the ninth a whole series of official missions were sent by sea to China. The Japanese cities of Nara and Kyoto were built on the same plan as Chang'an, though naturally smaller. The regular layout of Kyoto still remains today, and the best examples of Tang wooden architecture also survive in Japan rather than in China.

THE DESTRUCTION OF CHANG'AN

In the ninth century Chang'an's importance waned, with the Tang Dynasty itself coming under pressure as factions jostled for power. Twice Chang'an was sacked by peasant rebels and troops of the imperial forces. In AD 904 the Tang court was moved to Luoyang. The main surviving buildings were dismantled and the beams were taken to the Wei River where they were lashed together to form rafts which were floated down to the new capital. From AD 904–906 the city walls were demolished and a new, more modest, wall was built around the old Imperial City. In AD 907 the last Tang emperor was finally deposed and Chang'an was renamed Da'anfu.

THE IMPERIAL TOMBS OF THE TANG DYNASTY

From the tomb of the Emperor Xuanzong in the east to the tomb of Gaozong and Empress Wu in the west, the 18 Tang tombs are spread out in a line 120 kilometres

(75 miles) long. Most of them are set into natural hills and mountains, rather than underneath artificial mounds.

Each tomb was originally surrounded by a square wall and had a series of buildings for ceremonial purposes and for the use of the guards. Each had its own 'Spirit Way', an avenue lined with stone sculptures. The Tang conception was much grander than that of the Ming, as all 13 of the well-known Ming Tombs in Beijing share a common approach.

The underground palaces of the emperors remain untouched. Only the important subsidiary tombs of the Zhao Ling and Qian Ling have been excavated.

Sights

HUAQING HOT SPRINGS

A must for every visitor to Xi'an, Huaqing Hot Springs have been a favourite spa since the Tang Dynasty. For centuries emperors had come here to bathe and enjoy the scenic beauty. It remains an ideal spot for relaxation. The more energetic visitors may climb some or all of Li Mountain, on which are situated several Daoist (Taoist) and Buddhist temples. None of the buildings in the grounds are particularly important. Although many of them are named after Tang halls and pavilions, they were built either at the end of the last century or during this one.

Huaqing Hot Springs can be conveniently visited on returning from the Terracotta Army site. A principal pleasure spot for Chinese tourists, the place is nearly always packed, and especially so on Sundays.

The resort dates back to the Western Zhou when construction began on a series of pleasure resort palaces at the hot springs site, which is 30 kilometres (18 miles) from Xi'an, at the foot of Black Horse Mountain. The First Emperor of Qin had a residence there, as did Han Wudi, the Martial Emperor. In more recent times even Chiang Kai-shek used some of the buildings. However, the strongest associations are with the Tang: Black Horse Mountain is still covered with the pine and cypress trees planted by Tang Xuanzong, and the present buildings have a Tang atmosphere.

Taizong commissioned his architect Yan Lide (Yen Li-te) to design a palace, the Tangquan, in AD 644. It became the favourite resort of Xuanzong, who spent every winter there from AD 745 to 755 in the company of Yang Guifei, the Imperial Concubine (see page 78). The resort was greatly enlarged in AD 747 and renamed Huaqing Palace. The complex was destroyed at the end of the Tang.

However, imperial bathing pools from this period (AD 618–907), lost for almost a millennia, were discovered in 1982 by workmen renovating the Guifei Pavilion. They uncovered remains of palace architecture, including lotus-shaped roof tile-ends and four bathing pools—the Star, Long, Lotus and Guifei pools. The Guifei or Hibiscus pool, dating from AD 712–756, has now been restored and is open to the public—but for viewing, not for bathing. It is a terraced structure with a central, empty, pool in the shape of a Chinese crab-apple blossom. The fountainhead, designed to represent the stamens of a flower, is a reproduction of the original.

■ THE BATHS

The best way to appreciate the Huaqing Hot Springs is, of course, to take a bath. The water rises at a constant temperature of 43°C (109°F) and contains various minerals, including lime and manganese carbonate.

The baths are exotically named. The Lotus, the Crab Apple and the Emperor's Nine Dragon Bath, for example, can be hired by a couple for Rmb20 for one hour (the price includes soap, shampoo and the use of a towel). Communal baths are a bargain at 3 *mao* per soak if one does not mind mingling with 49 other bathers of the same sex. There are hot spring baths at the Huaqing Guesthouse (see page 137) but they are reserved for guests.

Marble boat and the Nine Dragon Pool at Huaqing Hot Springs

■ THE SITE OF THE XI'AN INCIDENT

The Five Chamber Building, just behind the Imperial Concubine's Bath, contains the bedroom used by Chiang Kai-shek on the eve of the Xi'an Incident of 1936—also known as the Double Twelfth Incident as it happened on 12th December (see page 104). As the rebellious troops of Zhang Xueliang showered the pavilion with gunfire, Chiang escaped through a window and over the back wall. The broken panes of the windows can still be seen. Chiang was captured many hours later on Li Mountain. His hiding place is now marked by an iron chain. The kiosk commemorating his capture was originally erected by the Nationalists to celebrate their leader's escape.

QIAN LING

Of all the imperial tomb complexes near Xi'an Qian Ling is probably the best pre-served and the most complete. It is the mausoleum of Emperor Tang Gaozang and Empress Wu Zetian (see page 66) and is situated 85 kilometres (53 miles) west of Xi'an. It has never been robbed or excavated but there are interesting relics in its vicinity.

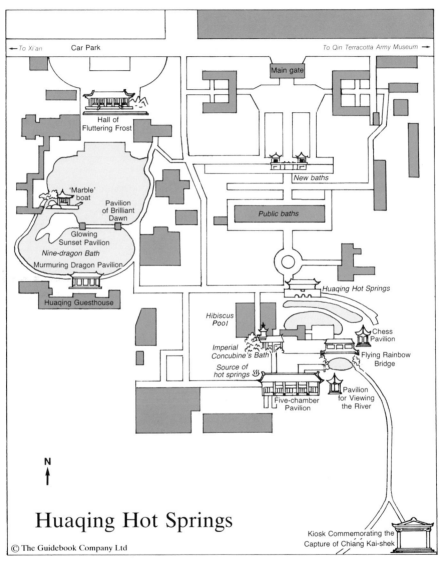

← To Xi'an   Car Park   To Qin Terracotta Army Museum →

Main gate

Hall of
Fluttering Frost

New baths

'Marble'
boat
Pavilion
of Brilliant
Dawn

Public baths

Glowing
Sunset Pavilion
Nine-dragon Bath
Murmuring Dragon Pavilion

Huaqing Hot Springs

Huaqing Guesthouse

Hibiscus
Pool

Chess
Pavilion

Imperial
Concubine's Bath

Flying Rainbow
Bridge

Source of
hot springs

Five-chamber
Pavilion

Pavilion
for Viewing
the River

N

Huaqing Hot Springs

© The Guidebook Company Ltd

Kiosk Commemorating the
Capture of Chiang Kai-shek

If you stand at the southern approach to the mausoleum you can appreciate the original Tang layout and design. This main southern approach is between two prominent small hills, surmounted with towers built in the eighth century. From a distance, the hills greatly resemble a pair of women's breasts, incurring the tale that

Emperor Tang Gaozang had them constructed to honour the natural beauty of his wife. Beneath them are two obelisk-like Cloud Pillars and then a series of pairs of stone statues lining the route to the mausoleum.

This grand and imposing avenue of animal and human statues leading all the way to the tombs is perhaps Qian Ling's most impressive feature, creating a memorable and awe-inspiring effect.

First there are two winged horses, then two vermilion birds like ostriches. Five pairs of saddled horses come next, originally each with a groom. These are followed by ten pairs of tall, almost hieratic guardians. They have very large heads, wear long-sleeved robes, and hold the hilts of long swords that rest on the ground in front of them.

Beyond the guardians are two stone memorials; the one on the left (west) commemorates the reign of Tang Gaozang and is balanced on the east side by the so-called Blank Tablet in honour of Empress Wu. The original implication was apparently that the old empress was beyond praise, but memorials were in fact inscribed on it during the Song and Jin dynasties (960–1234).

North of the two ruined towers is a remarkable collection of 61 stone figures, now headless. From the inscriptions on the backs of these figures it appears that they represent actual foreigners who came to the Chinese court in the seventh century; some were envoys of central Asian countries, others were barbarian chiefs. Behind them are two powerful sculptures of stone lions, guarding the southern entrance to the original inner enclosure, now no longer extant. There are similar pairs of animals at the north, east and west entrances. Just inside the old southern entrance is an 18th-century stele.

■ THE QIAN LING SATELLITE TOMBS

To the southeast of the principal mausoleum are 17 satellite tombs beneath man-made mounds. The names of the occupants are all known. Five of the tombs were excavated between 1960 and 1972. They had previously been robbed, but evidently only of gold, silver and precious gems. Archaeologists found a large number of pieces of pottery. But by far the most exciting discoveries at the sites were the mural paintings in the interiors. These provide valuable information about Tang court life, and are exquisite examples of the quality of the period's art.

Unfortunately the paintings started to deteriorate soon after the tombs had been opened. All the principal ones have now been taken to the Shaanxi History Museum and replaced with reproductions which are fairly accurate copies of the originals.

THE TOMB OF PRINCESS YONGTAI (YUNG-T'AI)

This was the first tomb to be excavated and remains the most impressive of all the

(following pages) Polo players, from a mural at Prince Zhanghuai's tomb, Qian Ling

YANG GUIFEI

Yang Guifei was a concubine whose love affair with Emperor Xuanzong of the Tang Dynasty eventually brought about his downfall and the collapse of Xi'an's Golden Era. Her renowned beauty, and her power, have become legendary in China.

When Emperor Xuanzong had firmly established a strong empire with a cosmopolitan capital in Xi'an and a brilliant court, he ordered a search throughout the land to find China's greatest beauty. Thousands of young women—one from as far away as Japan—are said to have been brought before him, only to be discarded or relegated to a secondary status in the back rooms of his palace.

One day, at Huaqing Hot Springs, Yang, the 18-year-old daughter of a high official and concubine of one of the emperor's many sons, caught Xuanzong's eye. Amidst protestations from his son, Xuanzong took Yang to be his own concubine, and she grew to yield enormous influence over the emperor, who began neglecting matters of state to spend time with her. He renamed her Yang Guifei—Yang the Imperial Concubine.

Tang-dynasty paintings indicate that—like other beauties of the time—Yang Guifei was as plump as a harem queen. Taking great pains to please her, the emperor had the palace at Huaqing Hot Springs enlarged, and she spent many languorous hours bathing there to keep her skin fresh. As the eminent Chinese poet Bai Juyi recounted:

> One cold spring day she was ordered
> To bathe in the Huaqing Palace baths,
> The warm water slipped down
> Her glistening jade-like body.
> When maids helped her rise
> She looked so frail and lovely,
> At once she won the emperor's favour. . .
> Behind the warm lotus-flower curtain,
> They took their pleasure in the spring nights,
> Regretting only that the nights were too short,
> Rising only when the sun was high,
> He stopped attending court sessions . . .

Constantly she amused and feasted with him,
Accompanying him on spring outings,
Spending every night with him.
Though many beauties were in the palace,
More than three thousand of them,
All his favours were centred on her.

(Translated by Yang Xianyi and Gladys Yang)

As Yang Guifei's spell over the emperor grew, so did her demands. Fresh lychees, her favourite fruit, were brought by pony express from the southern coastal city of Guangzhou every week. Many of her relatives took positions at court, with her cousin becoming Prime Minister.

Yang Guifei also caught the eye of a Mongolian Turk, An Lushan, who had become military governor in north China. Visiting the Tang court often, he was rumoured to have become Yang's lover. Although 15 years her elder, he was—in a bizarre ceremony—adopted as her son. An Lushan became impatient for power, and soon attempted a forceful takeover of the capital.

As his troops neared Xi'an, the emperor fled with Yang Guifei to the west. Years of neglect had weakened the imperial army, and its remaining soldiers were determined to remove Yang Guifei, whom they blamed for the military decline. When stopping to change horses at Mawei, the soldiers mutinied, killing the Prime Minister, and demanding that the 'moth-like eyebrows' of Yang Guifei be surrendered as well.

A more valiant lover might have given his own life first, but Xuanzong stood helplessly by as Yang Guifei was strangled in the courtyard of a small Buddhist temple. Her tomb is still there today.

The An Lushan rebellion dragged on for several years, but was eventually crushed. The emperor, however, never recovered from his loss of Yang Guifei, and he died a broken man a few years later. The Tang Dynasty survived nominally, but a steady decline had set in, and its former glory was never regained.

Betrayal

Three nights were required to open a shaft. Most commonly the main funeral passage lay directly below the earthen mound, and the crypt itself, containing the sarcophagus, lay at some remove. Sometimes, to confuse robbers, the main passage, the inner passage, and the crypt itself bore no relation at all to the external mound. The several cuts would wind and twist, and then the door to the crypt would be at the spot least expected. Sometimes it was by no means easy even to find the crypt. Incomparably more difficult was the task of getting the funeral treasures out. These were of course the tombs of the rich and noble. They had been devised on the assumption that there would be robbers . . . .

For three nights the ten of them took turns at digging. Some forty feet below the spot chosen by Ko they came upon a flat rock about a yard square which might have been called a skylight. The stone was too large for two or three men to move. Since they were confined to the narrow shaft they had opened, they were two nights making their way into the passage below. When finally they had succeeded, there was still a little time before daybreak. Some in the band wanted to proceed immediately, but Ch'ên said with some firmness that they would wait until the next night. Against possible discovery, they had yet to block the shaft and cover it with weeds. The secret of grave robbing was to leave time for everything.

It was a cloudy night of fierce winds when they finally made their way inside. The band seemed to gather from nowhere, work clothes beating in the wind. The season was neither warm nor cold. The light of the lanterns was now bright, now low.

Ch'ên looked from one to another. They were not to have thoughts of private booty, he said, they were to share alike. And he approached a young woman, the only woman among them, and a tall young man.

'You two will stand guard outside,' he said.

The woman was his third wife, the man his younger brother.

'Get inside, the rest of you.'

As if in a sort of ceremonial capacity as leader, he took up a lantern and bent over to enter the dark hold. Three men followed him and *mattocks and shovels and hammers and the like were brought down, and the other four disappeared inside.*

The darkness was more profound than on the surface. The only sound was the whistling of the wind. He had left as sentinels his wife and a brother with whom he shared the same blood, and in the choice had been considerations of a sort that Ch'ên would make. Had he chosen anyone else, he could not have been sure when the stone would be toppled back into place. The others were his trusted comrades, but they were human, and he could not be sure when temptation would raise its head. If the stone were to fall, if only that were to happen, then the men inside would not see the light of day again. Ten days would pass and they would lie dead of starvation, and the treasure would be the property of him who had betrayed them. The men in the tomb were always conscious, therefore, of who it was that stood watch outside. Though it was the usual thing for a relative of someone inside the tomb to be drafted for the work, that was not always the safest procedure. There were wives who cursed husbands, sons who hated fathers. Ch'ên's choice of his own wife and brother had much to recommend it to the others. Ch'ên's young wife got along well with her husband, and she was a good-natured, amiable woman, pleasant to everyone. The brother had been reared like a son. He was of a wholesome nature such as to deny that he and Ch'ên shared the same blood, and well thought of by everyone.

But it was not as wise a choice as the other thought it. The moment the two were alone the woman held out her hand to the man.

'Put the lid back on. Make up your mind to it. Go in and do it.'

She spoke in a low voice. The young man was startled. The same terrible thought had been with him from the moment he was appointed sentinel. He had been having an affair with the woman for a year and more. Though she was his brother's wife she did not seem like a sister-in-law. Ch'ên had taken advantage of the fact that she was without resources, and had as good as kidnapped her, and had his way with her.

There was a rustling as the youth went off through the grass. The woman followed.

Yasushi Inoue, 'Princess Yung-t'ai's Necklace' *from* Lou-lan and Other Stories, *translated by James T Araki & Edward Seidensticker*

Empress Wu

The Golden Age of the Tang Dynasty was ushered in not by an emperor but by an ex-concubine, who became the only woman sovereign in Chinese history. Wu Zhou's remarkable career began in AD 638 when she entered the palace, aged 13, as junior concubine to Emperor Taizong. On his death 11 years later she was relegated to a Buddhist nunnery, as custom dictated, but by then—so it is traditionally alleged—she had already become the mistress of his son, Gaozong. She returned to court as Gaozong's favourite concubine, set about arranging the murder of the empress and other female rivals, and within a few years gained the rank of imperial consort for herself. Her ascendancy was not achieved without the ruthless dispatch of many opponents—ministers who had enjoyed the emperor's trust, members of the imperial family, and all those courtiers who claimed that her friendship with Gaozong was incestuous.

For much of Gaozong's long reign (AD 649–83) real power was in the hands of Empress Wu. She fully exploited his weakness and her own skill for intrigue. Purges of rivals—who were murdered or exiled—kept her position secure, but historians agree that it could not have been sustained had she not possessed great intelligence and a genius for administration. Although she was whimsical, superstitious and highly susceptible to the flattery of any sorcerer and monk who could win her favour, she remained for most of her rule consistently adept at picking competent statesmen and military leaders to carry out her policies. The conquest of Korea and defeat of the Turks were accomplished during her time. The imperial examination system—by which government officials were chosen regardless of social standing—was promoted, so that in time political power was transferred from the aristocracy to a scholar-bureaucracy. She was, as one historian put it, 'not sparing in the bestowal of titles and ranks, because she wished to

tombs that can be seen. Princess Yongtai was a granddaughter of Emperor Gaozong and Empress Wu. She died in AD 701 at the age of 17.

The circumstances surrounding her death were mysterious. According to the records she was executed by her ruthless grandmother on suspicion of having criticized some court favourites. Five years after her death her remains were exhumed and her tomb built in the Qin Ling complex. The memorial tablet inside the tomb states she died in childbirth, perhaps because the manner of her actual death was considered shameful.

cage the bold and enterprising spirits of all regions . . . but those who proved unfit for their responsibilities were forthwith, in large numbers, cashiered or executed. Her broad aim was to select men of real talent and true virtue.' During her years in power the stability of the empire laid the foundation for the prosperity and cultural achievements that followed and culminated in the High Tang.

Empress Wu bore Gaozong four sons and one daughter. Their second son was named heir-apparent in AD 675 but Empress Wu, suspecting him of an attempted coup, banished the prince to Sichuan. It was there that he was subsequently made to take his own life, on his mother's orders. When the emperor died, another of Empress Wu's sons was enthroned. He proved to be as ineffectual as his father, and was speedily deposed and exiled as well. The reign of the next crown prince was equally short. In AD 690, Empress Wu dispensed with puppet emperors altogether by proclaiming a new dynasty—Zhou—and usurping the throne. Her title, Wu Zetian (Wu is Heaven), underscored her claim to the Mandate of Heaven.

While Wu Zetian continued to govern effectively, the last decade of her reign was overshadowed by several more savage murders. By now in her 70s, the old empress was becoming increasingly dependent on two corrupt courtiers, the Zhang brothers. Their malevolent presence was intensely loathed by the rest of the court, and it was insinuations against her favourites that impelled Wu Zetian to order the execution of her granddaughter, her step-grandson and another Wu relative on a charge of disloyalty. The Zhang brothers were finally killed in a palace coup in AD 705, which forced the empress to abdicate in favour of her exiled son and restore the Tang. She died less than a year later.

When the tomb was excavated, archaeologists came across an unexpected and gruesome discovery: the skeleton of a tomb robber, evidently murdered by his accomplices. The modern Japanese writer Yasushi Inoue has written a short story, *Princess Yung-tai's Necklace*, based on the incident (see page 80).

In contrast to all these chilling associations are the charming murals on the tunnel walls leading down to the princess's tomb. They represent court attendants, almost all of them women, wearing the elegant central Asian fashions of the day. The stone sarcophagus is also beautifully engraved with figures, birds and flowers. But it

is now empty. Archaeologists suspect that the princess's actual remains were buried secretly nearby, but they have never been found.

THE TOMB OF PRINCE YIDE (I-TE)

The tomb of Princess Yongtai's half-brother, who died at the age of 19, apparently executed for the same reason and at the same time as his half-sister, is dated the same year as hers, AD 706.

The ceiling of Prince Yide's tomb is decorated with stars, and the walls with court ladies and eunuchs, palace guards and hunting attendants. There is also a long mural at the entrance with a 196-man procession of guards massed below the high watchtowers of a palace.

(above) Tomb mural, Tang Dynasty

THE TOMB OF THE HEIR-APPARENT PRINCE ZHANGHUAI

Prince Zhanghuai was one of Empress Wu's sons and he too fell foul of this formidable lady. He was heir-apparent from AD 675 to 680, but was then disgraced by his mother and forced to commit suicide in AD 684, at the age of 31. His tomb was built in about AD 706. The two main paintings in the tomb are of a polo match on one side, and a hunting cavalcade on the other. There are also representations of foreign emissaries with court officials.

The two other tombs that have been opened are of the Prime Minister Xue Yuanzhao and General Li Jinxing, and are of lesser importance.

ZHAO LING

Zhao Ling is the tomb of Emperor Taizong, who founded the Tang Dynasty. It is located in the main peak of Mount Jiuzong, approximately 60 kilometres (40 miles) northwest of Xi'an. Although 14 of the satellite tombs have been excavated, the emperor's mausoleum itself has not. The whole necropolis covers an area of some 20,000 hectares (78 square miles). Visitors are normally taken to see **Zhao Ling Museum**, but not the site on Mount Jiuzong itself.

Taizong was a great military commander who loved horses. Six bas-reliefs of his favourite mounts including his most famous horse, Quanmo, were originally placed at the northern entrance to the tomb. Considered masterpieces of Tang sculpture, they are unfortunately no longer *in situ*. The Quanmo stone, together with one other, was taken to the University Museum of Philadelphia in 1914. The other four stones are in the Stone Sculpture Gallery of the Shaanxi Museum, along with plaster reproductions of the two in America. The originals were broken in several places in 1918, apparently in an attempt to facilitate their transport abroad.

The museum displays all the artifacts removed from the excavated satellite tombs. There is a splendid selection of Tang funerary pottery, both glazed and unglazed, including figurines of Chinese and central Asians, horses and camels. There are some fragments of wall paintings, a ceremonial crown from a satellite tomb and a massive pottery roof finial from the Hall of Offerings, the main building of the original enclosure in front of the emperor's mausoleum.

The museum also features a Forest of Steles (not to be confused with the famous one at Shaanxi Museum). This is a collection of 42 vertical memorial tablets which originally stood outside the tomb mounds, together with ten flat tablets from the interiors.

Unfortunately, the majority of the thousands of laboriously etched characters on these steles are illegible. They were damaged by vandals in the contemporary Tang and succeeding Song dynasties who, having made rubbings of the inscriptions, sought to inflate the value of their paper copies by defacing the source tablets.

XINGQING PARK

This is the most pleasant park in Xi'an. Located east of the city wall's southeast corner, it is quiet and full of trees. On weekdays it is an excellent place to get away from the crowds.

The park was originally the site of a Tang palace, where the sons of Emperor Tang Ruizong (reigned AD 684–690, AD 710–712) lived at the beginning of the eighth century. It became known as the Xingqing Palace in AD 714 after Emperor Xuanzong succeeded his father.

Famous for its peonies, Xingqing was a favourite palace of Emperor Xuanzong and Imperial Concubine Yang. After the Tang, the land on which the palace had been built eventually reverted to agricultural use.

The transformation of the site into a park came about in 1958 during the Great Leap Forward. Thousands of citizens were involved in laying out the park, taking only 120 days to complete the 50-hectare (122-acre) project.

It has an ornamental lake and a number of Tang-style buildings bearing the names of famous halls and pavilions in the palace of Xuanzong. There is also a white marble memorial, erected in 1979, to Abe no Nakamaro (AD 701–770), a famous secular Japanese visitor to Chang'an during the Tang, who rose to become Collator of Texts in the Imperial Library.

REMAINS OF DAMING PALACE

Daming Palace, or the Palace of Great Luminosity, was begun by Taizong in AD 634 for the use of his father, although Gaozu died before it was completed. In AD 663 it was enlarged for Emperor Gaozang and from then on became the principal palace of the Tang emperors.

The site of Daming Palace is to the northwest of the walled city, on the fringe of the modern urban area. It is now largely fields. The terraces on which once stood Hanyuan Hall (where important ceremonies were held) and Linde Hall (another large, but informal complex) may still be seen, together with a depression which was the ornamental Penglai Pool in Tang times. The whole area was excavated between 1957 and 1959, and the foundations of some 20 buildings were discovered. The Linde Hall in particular was completely excavated, although the site had now been filled in again.

THE TANG DYNASTY ARTS MUSEUM

Situated in the shadow of the Big Goose Pagoda, the Tang Dynasty Arts Museum is an offshoot of the Sino-Japanese joint venture hotel, the Xi'an Garden or Tanghua Fandian. It consists of four exhibition halls.

Hall 1, which is devoted to the theme of 'Chang'an—the capital of the Tang

Dynasty', displays models of Daming Palace (see previous page) and other buildings. A map of the city compares its layout with those of contemporary Rome (at the western end of the Silk Road) and Alexandria in Egypt, and shows how those two metropolises were dwarfed by Chang'an at the time.

Hall 2 shows the prevailing style of dress, and grooming and social customs, with interesting information on women's hairdos, make-up and clothing. In Hall 3, the calligraphy, painting and chronicles of the Tang Dynasty are displayed.

There are various antiquities, primarily sculptures and murals, in Hall 4. However, you will see similar or better exhibits in the Shaanxi History Museum. An annexe on the right, the Lecture Room, highlights the strong influence of Tang-dynasty culture, art and customs on Japan, with references to similarities in language, coinage, clothing, hairstyles and food.

This is a place to enjoy relative peace and quiet amongst elegant exhibition halls laid out between attractive gardens. It is open to the public 9 am–5 pm.

Buddhism during and after the Tang

Background

During the Tang, Chang'an became the main centre for Buddhist learning in east Asia. The first contacts between adherents of Buddhism and the Chinese were probably made with the opening of the Silk Road during the reign of the Martial Emperor, Han Wudi (reigned 140–86 BC). During the following centuries this central Asian route, with Chang'an as its eastern terminus, remained the principal one by which Buddhism reached China.

Today a number of monuments bear witness to the importance of Buddhism in the city's history. Most famous are the two prominent landmarks with unforgettable names: the Big and the Little Goose Pagodas (see pages 90 and 91). Also in reasonable condition is Da Cien Temple (of which the Big Goose Pagoda is a part), and two interesting temples south of the city, the Xingjiao and the Xiangji Temples (see pages 94 and 97). Some other Buddhist temples have survived in various states of disrepair but may prove worth visiting, as much for the setting and the journey there as for the temple buildings themselves.

Several of the surviving temples and pagodas have particular associations with Buddhist monks, scholars and translators who made the journey from Chang'an to India in search of enlightenment, the Buddhist scriptures and, perhaps, adventure. Some 200 Chinese monks are recorded as travelling from Chang'an to India between the third and eighth centuries. A number of central Asian and Indian monks also came to Chang'an, but they are less well documented than the Chinese travellers.

Of these monks the best known is Xuanzang (Hsuan-tsang) who is today the most popular figure in the whole history of Chinese Buddhism. The Tang monk, as he is often simply called, is the hero of the long 16th-century Chinese novel *Pilgrimage to the West*, sometimes known as *Monkey*, which is loosely based on Xuanzang's travels. A scholar and translator, Xuanzang made a 17-year journey which took him to Nalanda (near Patna), then the greatest centre of Buddhist learning in India.

On his return he became abbot of Da Cien Temple (see page 90), where he spent the rest of his life working on translations of the Buddhist texts that he had brought with him from India. His remains were interred under a pagoda which is part of the Xingjiao Temple (see page 94).

By the early eighth century, Chang'an had a total of 64 monasteries and 27 nunneries. Much of the scholarship that resulted in the development of two important Buddhist sects—Pure Land and True Word—took place in the city. But the monasteries fulfilled a number of different roles, not only translating, studying and propa-

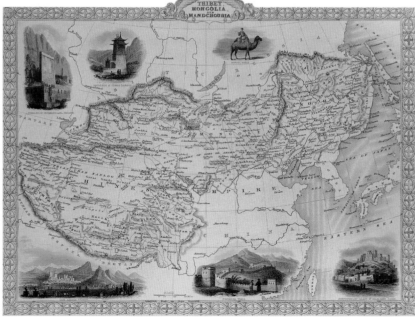

Among the most significant innovations carried along the old Silk Road to China was Buddhism.
Thibet, Mongolia and Mandchouria, *John Tallis, c. 1851 (above); China, Bellin, 1748 (below)*

gating religion, but also patronizing the arts, providing accommodation and even offering some banking facilities. They grew extremely rich, and Buddhism began to enjoy immense popularity at every level of society.

The Tang emperors, however, were ambivalent in their support of the foreign religion. They claimed that Laozi (Lao-tzu), the founder of China's indigenous religion Daoism (Taoism), was their ancestor. Increasingly the success of the great temple-monasteries provoked resistance, and attempts were made to limit their power and wealth. Finally in AD 841 came a crackdown: the insane Daoist Emperor Tang Wuzong ordered the dissolution of the monasteries and the return of monks and nuns to secular life. During the following four years, widespread Buddhist persecution led to the destruction of almost all the temple-monasteries. Though many of them were refounded after AD 845, and some of them survive to this day, Buddhism never completely recovered in China. And so, after the destruction of Chang'an at the end of the Tang, the city lost its position as a centre of Buddhist learning for good.

Sights

THE BIG GOOSE PAGODA AND DA CIEN TEMPLE

The Big Goose Pagoda (Dayan Ta), perhaps the most beautiful building left in Xi'an today, is one of the city's most distinctive and outstanding landmarks. The adjacent Da Cien Temple is the city's best-preserved Buddhist temple complex.

Situated 4 kilometres (2.5 miles) south of the walled city at the end of Yanta Lu, or Goose Pagoda Road, the temple and pagoda are on the sites of an earlier Sui temple. Da Cien Temple was established in AD 647 by Li Zhi (who became Emperor Tang Gaozong in AD 649) in memory of his mother Empress Wende.

Completed in AD 652, the pagoda was built at the request of the Tang monk, Xuanzang, whose pilgrimage to India is immortalized in the 16th-century Chinese novel *Pilgrimage to the West* or *Monkey*. Xuanzang asked Emperor Gaozong to build a large stone stupa like those he had seen on his travels. The emperor offered a compromise brick structure of five storeys, about 53 metres (175 feet) high, which was completed in AD 652. Originally called the Scripture Pagoda, it is said to be where Xuanzang translated into Chinese the Buddhist scriptures he brought back from India. Its present name, Big Goose Pagoda, has never been satisfactorily explained.

Between AD 701 and AD 704, at the end of the reign of Empress Wu, five more storeys were added to the pagoda, giving a sharper, more pointed form than it has today. Later damage, probably by fire, reduced it to the seven storeys it now has. It is a simple, powerful, harmonious structure, although ironically not how Xuanzang wanted it to be.

The pagoda rises 64 metres (210 feet) to the north of the other temple buildings, and is the only remaining Tang building in the complex. On the pedestal, at the entrance to the first storey, are some rather faded photographs providing a useful and fascinating survey of other famous pagodas in China, as well as a number of Tang inscriptions and engravings set in the base of the pagoda. There are some delightful tendril designs in bas-relief on the borders of the tablets and at the top of the tablets some exquisite coiling dragons and singing angels.

At the southern entrance of the pagoda are copies of prefaces to the translations of Xuanzang by the emperors Taizong and Gaozong in the calligraphy of Chu Sui-liang. Over the lintel of the western entrance is an engraving of Sakyamuni and other Buddhist figures. Some tablets, inscribed during the Ming (1368–1644), recount the exploits of the Tang monk. On a fine day climb up inside the internal wooden staircase to the top of the pagoda for a panoramic view.

During the Tang, Da Cien Temple was a considerable establishment. There were about 300 resident monks and no fewer than 1,897 rooms around 13 courtyards. It contained paintings by the leading artists of the day, and had the finest peony garden in the capital.

Although the temple was one of four to continue functioning after the great Buddhist persecution of AD 841–845, it was destroyed at the end of the Tang (AD 907). Since then it has been ruined and restored several times, but on a diminished scale. The last major restoration occurred in 1954, when the pagoda pedestal was widened.

The temple entrance is on the south side. Outside is a stone lamp from the Japanese city of Kyoto. Inside, to the right and left, are the Bell and Drum Towers, and a path leading to the Great Hall. This contains three statues of buddhas, surrounded by 18 clay figures of Sakyamuni Buddha's disciples. Both the building and the statues inside are said to date from 1466. To the east of the Great Hall are several small stone pagodas marking the remains of monks of the Qing period (1644–1911).

The temple is open from 8.30 am to 6 pm.

THE LITTLE GOOSE PAGODA AND DA JIANFU TEMPLE

The Little Goose Pagoda (Xiaoyan Ta) is one of Xi'an's major landmarks. Situated to the south of the walled city, the 13-storey eighth-century pagoda is all that remains of the once flourishing Da Jianfu Temple. The temple, established in AD 684 in honour of Emperor Gaozong, was particularly associated with pilgrim Yijing (I-ching), who settled there in the early eighth century to translate texts he had brought back from India. Although the temple continued to function after the Buddhist persecutions of AD 841–845, everything was destroyed save the Little Goose Pagoda, and an old locust tree said to have been planted during the Tang. Later, more modest temple buildings were erected next to the pagoda.

On Climbing the Big Goose Pagoda[1] in Chang'an

At the top of the pagoda one feels
To have truly entered the sky;
Wind drums incessantly; I am
Not one free of care and here my worry increases; and
  this structure,
Representing the power of Buddha,
Makes one wish to understand
And penetrate the depths of his secrets;
Looking through the dragon and snake
Openings, one marvels at their intricacy
Of construction; the seven
Stars come into view and the Milky Way;
One knows that the sun has been forced down,
And that it is autumn already; clouds
Obscure the mountain; the waters
Of the clear Wei and the muddy Ching[2]
Seem to have come together; below us
Is the mist, so can one hardly realize
Down there lies our capital;
There is a hardly-to-be-defined air
Near the grave of the ancient Emperor Shun,
And one cries for his awakening; but now
By the Jade Lake, the Queen of the Western
Heavens disports herself with wine, as
The sun sets behind Mount Kunlun
And yellow cranes fly aimlessly,
While the wild geese stream into
The sunset, searching for life.

Du Fu (712–770)

1 Du Fu with some other poets on an excursion to the Pagoda of Kindness and Grace, better
   known now as the 'Dayan Ta' or 'Big Goose Pagoda', still standing in modern Xi'an.
2 The Wei and the Ching, names of two rivers in the northwest of China; one was always clear
   while the other was muddy even after their confluence. Today both are muddy.

The Big Goose Pagoda

The pagoda has not survived completely unscathed. When it was completed in AD 707 the brick structure had 15 storeys, but it was damaged during a series of earthquakes in the late 15th and 16th centuries. In 1487, the pagoda was split from top to bottom by the impact of an earthquake measuring 6.25 on the Richter scale. Amazingly, it did not fall. In 1556 another quake, 8 on the Richter scale, had its epicentre some 75 kilometres (47 miles) east of Xi'an. This one had the effect of throwing the two sides of the pagoda together again, but it also dislodged the top two storeys.

The Little Goose Pagoda has remained to this day only 13 storeys, 43 metres (141 feet) high. There have been conflicting opinions about the original appearance of the building (models of different designs are on display at the temple), which is partly why a complete restoration has never been attempted. Meanwhile, however, the slightly crumbling, open part of its apex gives it a distinct style. A new internal staircase was put up in 1965 so you can climb right to the top and look out over the fields to the walled city to the north. Unlike the Big Goose Pagoda, which has only narrow windows, here you can climb out to an open roof to enjoy an untrammelled view of the surroundings.

Among the noteworthy features of the pagoda are some Tang-period engravings of bodhisattvas on the stone lintels at its base. There is also a tablet commemorating a restoration of the pagoda in 1116 and another engraved during the Qing (1644–1911) with information about the earthquakes. A stone tablet dated 1692 gives an interesting idea of what the temple and pagoda would have looked like at that date, except that the pagoda is represented with 15 storeys.

Standing in one of the courtyards is a large bell, cast in 1192 in Wugong County, west of Xi'an, and moved to the temple about five centuries later. Traditionally a Buddhist monk struck a bell before noon and a drum in the afternoon and evening. A drum stands opposite the bell, but visitors will have to imagine their sounds.

It is worth visiting the exhibition rooms of Shaanxi handicrafts at this pagoda. The Little Goose pagoda is open from 8.30 am to 5.30 pm.

XINGJIAO TEMPLE

This temple is in a very pleasant setting, overlooking the Fanchuan River, 22 kilometres (14 miles) southwest of Xi'an, just beyond the village of Duqu. Xingjiao Temple, or the Temple of the Flourishing Teaching, was one of the Eight Great Temples of Fanchuan. It was built in AD 669 by Tang Gaozong as a memorial to the Tang monk Xuanzang (see page 88), together with a tall brick pagoda covering his ashes. The temple was restored in AD 828, though by AD 839 it again lay abandoned according to the inscription on Xuanzang's pagoda. However, it managed to survive until the 19th century when all the buildings were destroyed except the main pagoda and two smaller ones belonging to two of Xuanzang's disciples. The temple was again rebuilt, partly in 1922, partly in 1939. Today, over 30 monks live and worship there.

The three pagodas stand in a walled enclosure called Cien Pagoda Courtyard. The tall central pagoda is dedicated to Xuanzang. It is a beautiful five-storey brick structure, with brackets in relief, in imitation of the old wooden-style pagodas. It probably dates from the ninth century. A small pavilion next to the pagoda has a modern copy of a stone engraving of Xuanzang, carrying the scriptures in what might be described as a sutra-backpack.

On either side of the principal pagoda are those of Xuanzang's two translation assistants. Each is of three storeys. On the east side is that of Kuiji (K'uei-chi, AD 632–682), nephew of General Yuchi Jingde (a general of Emperor Tang Taizong). It was erected during the Tang. On the other side stands the pagoda of Yuance (Yuan-ts'e), a Korean follower of Xuanzang. This was built later, in 1115.

At the entrance to the complex are the Bell and Drum Towers. These are 20th-century constructions but retain the original instruments from the 19th century or earlier. Facing the entrance is the Great Hall of the Buddha, built in 1939, which contains a bronze, Ming-period Buddha. The Preaching Hall behind was built in 1922 and contains a number of statues including a bronze, Ming-period Amitabha Buddha and a Sakyamuni Buddha of the same date as the hall.

In the eastern courtyard is the two-storey library, built in 1922 and restored in 1939. It contains a white jade Buddha from Burma. The library proper is on the upper floor and possesses some Tang-dynasty sutras, written in Sanskrit, as well as 20th-century editions of the great Tang translations of Xuanzang and others.

You can reach the temple by bus number 215 that leaves from Xi'an's South Gate. The trip takes about 40 minutes.

DAXINGSHAN TEMPLE
Daxingshan Temple was the greatest Buddhist establishment of the Sui and Tang, but since the tenth century it has been destroyed and rebuilt several times. The latest reconstruction was in 1956. Today its grounds have been turned into a small, quiet and charming park (Xinfeng Park). The main buildings have been repainted, and a handful of monks live and worship there.

The temple is said to date back to the third century when it was known as the Zunshan Temple. It was refounded during the Sui when it was given its present name, and became the headquarters of an order with a network of 45 prefectural temples, all established Yang Qian, founder of the Sui Dynasty. During the Tang it became a great centre of Buddhist art and learning and the Tang monk, Xuanzang, hero of the famous Chinese novel *Monkey*, stayed there during the seventh century. Most of the buildings were destroyed during the Buddhist persecution of 841–845,

Funerary Finery

In a large grey building standing to one side of the Drum Tower, under a line of Chinese characters painted to read 'Municipal Theatre Costume Retail Department', there was a door with a curious sign on its lintel. It said: 'Funeral and Interment Clothes Sold Here'. The door was closed, but you could get into the shop by either one of two additional entrances; these had signs which said, 'Men's and Women's Fashions', and 'Theatrical Costumes, Props and Dance Costumes.'

I thought that this was worth more than a moment of my curiosity, and stepped into the darkness of the building. I made for the funeral clothes counter, which turned out to be in the far end of the shop. It was very dark there, but still it was not difficult to see the sign pinned up above the counter, which said, 'Burial suits, once sold, are without exception not returnable'. I asked to see one.

She took a minute to look through her stock—from where I stood I could see that she was plentifully supplied—and came up with something which I thought you nowadays only saw in the movies. It took my breath away, it was so sumptuous, a beautiful ensemble in silk, such as might have been worn by a court lady in the Qing dynasty. The robe was of purple silk, deep as the skin of an aubergine, and trimmed with a border of gold. The skirt, of a heavier silk, was midnight blue and splashed with a phoenix pattern embroidered in gold. (I supposed that the male version would be a dragon.) Together the pieces cost 32 yuan, well over half of an average wage earner's monthly salary.

In such finery are the richer dead arrayed when they go to their graves in China. How incorrigible they are, those millions of Chinese in their baggy blue suits; if they don't dress very stylishly when they are alive they certainly make up for it when they die. And the thought came to me that all the chic, all the colour, all the money of China is expended on the children and the dead.

Lynn Pan, China's Sorrow

and whatever survived disappeared at the end of the Tang. The temple was rebuilt under the Ming and again restored in 1785 by an expert on Tang-dynasty Chang'an called Bi Yuan (1730–97). After its reconstruction in 1956 it was used by a community of Lamaist monks until the Cultural Revolution (1966–76). Today it houses the Xi'an Buddhist Association.

The temple and Xinfeng Park are located south of the Little Goose Pagoda on a small street called Xingshan Si Jie, behind the open market of Xiaozhai.

XIANGJI TEMPLE

Xiangji Temple, which has an 11-storey pagoda built in AD 706, lies due south of Xi'an some 20 kilometres (12 miles), close to the town of Wangqu. The square brick pagoda was built over the ashes of the Buddhist Shandao, one of the patriarchs of Pure Land Buddhism which preached salvation through faith rather than meditation. It was built by a disciple named Jingye, who is himself commemorated by a smaller five-storey brick pagoda nearby. Around the pagodas were originally the buildings of one of the great temple-monasteries of Tang Chang'an, although these have long since disappeared.

The pagoda of Shandao is similar in some respects to that of Xuanzang at the Temple of Flourishing Teaching. It has brackets in relief and imitates a wooden structure. If you want to climb the pagoda, try persuading one of the monks for permission. There are about 25 monks who now live and worship at the temple.

On 14 May 1980, which was, by Chinese reckoning, the 1,300th anniversary of Shandao's death in AD 681, a major restoration of the temple was completed. The Great Hall of the Buddha was rebuilt, and a Japanese Buddhist delegation presented a figure of the monk Shandao. It is now on view inside the hall together with a figure of Amitabha Buddha which was brought from a Beijing museum.

It is difficult to reach the temple by public transport and the journey may take over two hours. Bus number 215 leaves you at a village 6.4 kilometres (4 miles) from the temple, and from there you have to take a second bus which runs irregularly, or walk. But the beautiful surrounding countryside and, of course, the pagodas themselves make the trip well worthwhile.

CAOTANG TEMPLE

Sometimes translated as the Straw Hut Temple, Caotang Temple was founded during the Tang. Surrounded by fields, it lies about 55 kilometres (35 miles) southwest of Xi'an.

The temple was built on the site of a palace where Kumarajiva, a fourth-century translator of Buddhist scriptures, once worked and taught. Kumarajiva's translations, known for their elegant style rather than for their accuracy, have been used continuously down to modern times. The ashes of Kumarajiva are beneath a stone stupa, thought to be Tang, about two metres (6.5 feet) high, inside a small pavilion. In front there are some old cypress trees and a well. Other temple buildings include bell and tablet pavilions and a main hall.

Located on the road to Huxian, the temple is accessible by taxi or long-distance bus.

HUAYAN TEMPLE

Huayan Temple was founded by the first patriarch of the Huayan sect of Buddhism, the monk Dushan (Tu-shun, AD 557–640), during the reign of Tang Taizong. In its heyday, the Huayan Temple, situated in the Fanchuan area 20 kilometres (12 miles) south of Xi'an, was one of the Eight Great Temples of Fanchuan which flourished during the Tang.

Today, the only part of the temple to have survived are two brick pagodas on the side of the hill. One of them is 23 metres (75 feet) high and is square, like Big Goose Pagoda, with seven storeys; the other is smaller with four storeys and is hexagonal in form. There is a good view of the surrounding area from the pagodas.

Located on the road that passes through Chang'an, southeast of Xi'an, the pagodas are accessible by bus number 215 that leaves from the South Gate (a trip of about 45 minutes) and can be visited conveniently on the way to Xingjiao Temple.

THE TEMPLE OF THE RECUMBENT DRAGON

The Temple of the Recumbent Dragon, believed to be of Sui foundation, was served by some 300 monks during the Ming Dynasty (1368–1644). It suffered particularly badly during the Cultural Revolution (1966–76), when virtually all the artwork was destroyed as everything but the strongest walls and foundations were razed to the ground.

For almost two decades the temple site was used to house a factory. Now, three-quarters of the floor area has been returned to the temple's jurisdiction in compliance with Government policy promoting freedom of religious beliefs. Since 1985, forty-eight monks have been assigned to the temple, and three large halls and several peripheral structures have been built.

The first two large halls are for Buddhist worship and rites, while the third functions more practically as a dining hall, furnished simply with four refectory tables. Access to the temple is down a lane between numbers 25 and 27 Baishulin Jie, close to the Shaanxi Museum.

GUANGREN TEMPLE

The Guangren Temple is a Lama temple, located on Xibei Yi Lu within the north-westernmost corner of the city wall. It is one of only four such temples outside Tibet, the others being the Labrang Lamasery in southern Gansu, the Ta'er Lamasery in Qinghai, and the Lama Temple in Beijing. Built in 1705 during the Qing Dynasty, Guangren Temple functioned as a place of worship and lodging for monks and pilgrims travelling between Beijing and Tibet. According to the monks now serving at the temple, the Dalai Lama himself once stayed here briefly in 1952.

As with most religious sites during the catastrophic Cultural Revolution, Guangren Temple suffered from officially sanctioned destruction by Red Guards. A new temple on the original site has been built and opened to the public.

The temple is easily accessible for those travellers who circumnavigate the wall along the lane within the structure's shadow. Alternatively, you can get there by bus number 10, alighting at Yuxiang Men. Walk back east to Lianhu Lu, turn left into Xibei Yi Lu and the temple is at the end of the street against the wall.

FAMEN TEMPLE

Faman Temple is situated some 118 kilometres (73 miles) west of Xi'an, at a site on the Silk Road en route to Baoji, Tianshui and Lanzhou. It will thus appeal to travellers who are journeying west to retrace that ancient trade route, or indeed those visitors to Xi'an who can fit—just about—Famen Temple into a day's tour to the west which also encompasses Qian Ling, Zhao Ling, Mao Ling and the Xianyang Museum. Others may consider that the opportunity of seeing a supposed finger bone of the founder of Buddhism warrants a special day trip in itself, despite the two-and-a-half-hour taxi ride and fare in excess of 200 *yuan*.

The origins of the Famen Temple can be traced back to around AD 200, although its pagoda, a handsome 47-metre (154-foot)-high greyish-white brick octagonal structure with 13 levels, actually dates from Ming times.

About a century after the death of Sakyamuni, the founder of Buddhism, the ancient Indian King Ashoka decided to distribute a selection of Sakyamuni's relics to many places in the known world where Buddhism had gained adherents. Famen Temple was awarded a relic, a single finger bone. The original stupa, the structure built to house the precious relic, was thought to have been an earthen mound, then a wooden four-storey structure, but eventually the relic was moved to the crypt of the pagoda. During the Tang Dynasty, when the emperors and their concubines either came to Famen themselves or had the relic taken to Chang'an, the temple gained nationwide fame.

Later, when Buddhism was under wide attack (see page 90), an imperial edict ordered that the finger bone of Sakyamuni be destroyed. The relic was hidden by the monks, and as time passed it was believed to be lost until one day in 1987 when eight caskets containing several bones were discovered in the crypt beneath the pagoda's foundations.

All these bones (tiny, white in colour and tubular in shape), the jewel-encrusted precious metal caskets in which they were found, and hosts of other relics discovered at Famen are now on display in the Treasure Hall of the temple.

Period Five: Medieval and Modern Xi'an

Background

With the destruction of Chang'an at the end of the Tang, the city lost its political splendour and power for good. Thereafter it remained a regional centre, usually out of the mainstream of political developments. The real economic centre of China had already moved away from Chang'an, further to the southwest, during the late Tang. After AD 907 the Xi'an area became progressively more impoverished and culturally backward. Much of the history in the following millennium is a dismally repetitious account of droughts and floods, famines and peasant insurrections.

However, Daoism continued to find adherents and remnants of Daoist temples (see pages 124–125) can be seen in Xi'an today, despite the destruction caused during the Cultural Revolution. Islam, which had first been introduced into Chang'an by Arab merchants during the Tang, also flourished. Xi'an's beautiful Great Mosque is still functioning and welcomes foreign visitors (see page 121).

Between the fall of the Tang and the establishment of the Ming Dynasty in 1368, the city changed its name many times. In 1368 the city was renamed Xi'an Fu, the Prefecture of Western Peace. It was to remain as Xi'an from then on, except for the last year of the Ming Dynasty (1644), when the peasant leader Li Zicheng captured the city and renamed it Chang'an. (The name Chang'an survives today as the name of the county town immediately south of Xi'an.)

THE MING DYNASTY

In 1370 Zhu Yuanzhang, the first emperor of the Ming Dynasty, put his second son, Zhu Shuang, in control of Xi'an. Zhu Shuang became Prince of Qin, using the old name for the area. A palace was constructed for him and the city substantially rebuilt on the site of the Imperial City section of the Tang capital, covering approximately one sixth of the area of the former city. The prince did not take up residence until 1378, when the palace and the walls and gates of the city had already been completed. The palace, which was in the northeast part of the city, no longer exists but much of the 14th-century Xi'an still survives, notably the Bell and Drum towers and the city wall and gates.

THE QING DYNASTY

When the Manchus established the last imperial dynasty of China, the Qing, in 1644, Xi'an was garrisoned by Manchu troops. They occupied the northeast section of the city, which was walled off. In European accounts, these soldiers were referred to, inaccurately, as 'Tartars'.

Shaanxi farmer

THE XI'AN INCIDENT

Xi'an has always been known to the Chinese as a city rich with history, but it only gained recognition in much of the Western world in 1936 when Generalissimo Chiang Kai-shek was kidnapped there by some of his own generals.

The Xi'an Incident, as it became known, held the leadership of China hanging in the balance for a couple of tension-wracked weeks. An intriguing sequence of events brought on the kidnapping and its solution.

In 1936, while Hitler marched in Europe, the Japanese army was steadily tightening its grip on China. Chiang Kai-shek was not so much in control as simply being at the top of a fragile coalition of Chinese warlords and armies spread over China. The communists had escaped Chiang's pursuit on the Long March and established themselves securely at Yan'an, in the mountains north of Xi'an.

Chiang knew that a head-on conflict with the Japanese army would, if not demolish him, at least weaken his position, and make him vulnerable to the communists. He decided to appease the Japanese instead, and send many of his troops to fight the communists.

But for Zhang Xueliang, one of Chiang's allied generals, this policy of foot-dragging against the Japanese was unacceptable. A bright and courageous young general, Zhang was head of a Manchurian army and was incensed at the way his home in northeast China had been overrun by the Japanese since 1931. Zhang saw the situation deteriorating further in 1936, when the Japanese made a dramatic attack into Suiyan, a key area north of Beijing. On 4 December, a Nationalist attack on the communists failed, resulting in a widespread refusal amongst Chiang's troops to continue fighting. Chiang flew to Xi'an to direct the campaign himself.

Zhang saw this as an ideal moment to make a move. He discreetly made contact with the communists and at dawn on 12 December, his troops surrounded the palace at Huaqing Hot Springs, where Chiang was quar-

During the 18th century the city, or at least its officials and merchants, enjoyed some prosperity, as indicated by the great development of Qingqiang opera at this time (see page 30). However, the 19th century was less happy with natural calamities following fast behind a disastrous Muslim rebellion (1862–73).

In 1900 Xi'an again became a capital of sorts during the Boxer Rebellion when the Empress Dowager Cixi (Tz'u-hsi, 1835–1908), with her captive nephew, the power-

tered. Hearing gunfire, Chiang escaped barefoot in his nightshirt—leaving his dentures behind—scaled a wall, injuring his back, and scurried up an old path on Black Horse Mountain. Thirty of his men were killed defending him.

Zhang's officers combed the area, and one of them found their Generalissimo later that afternoon, shivering and in pain, crouched in a crevice between the rocks. As the officer moved to bind Chiang's hand, the Generalissimo reminded his captor that he was the Commander-in-Chief. The officer is said to have bowed politely to Chiang and replied, 'You are also our prisoner'.

Two weeks of tough negotiations followed. Chiang and his formidable wife, Soong May-ling, were on one side, with Zhang and Zhou Enlai, later communist China's Premier, on the other, while the rest of China waited impatiently. Many of the communist leaders wanted to execute Chiang, or at least keep him imprisoned. But a cable arrived from Moscow with an order from Stalin to release Chiang and get on with the task of fighting the Japanese.

The Chinese communists bristled at being told by 'Uncle Joe' how to handle what they saw as their own affair. But they also knew they could win some useful concessions out of Chiang if they released him.

In the end, a compromise was reached. Chiang was allowed to fly back to Nanjing a free man, but had to give up the pretence of being the sole leader of China. Ostensibly he joined with the communists in a 'National Front' against the Japanese. Zhang Xueliang, who also went back to Nanjing, was a hero only temporarily and was soon arrested by Chiang and branded a traitor.

The visitor to Huaqing Hot Springs can still see the site of this famous incident. The rooms where Chiang stayed and worked are marked, as is the spot up the hill where the Generalissimo was actually caught. The hiding place is marked by a chain and nearby, commemorating the capture, is a kiosk of dignified Grecian structure.

less Emperor Guangxu (Kuang-hsu), fled in disguise from Beijing. They stayed for over a year in Xi'an, beyond the reach of the Western powers, while peace was negotiated.

In 1911 when a nationwide revolution overthrew the Qing regime, resistance by the garrison in Xi'an collapsed without much of a struggle. But a terrible massacre of the Manchus ensued. Between 10,000 and 20,000 were killed, including a few un-

(following pages) Rapeseed fields outside Xi'an

lucky foreigners. Most of the buildings in the Manchu quarter were burned down. Such blood-letting and destruction did not occur in other cities. Much of the killing in Xi'an was evidently executed by the Muslims, in revenge for the suppression of their rebellion 40 years earlier.

XI'AN IN THE REPUBLICAN ERA

During the Republican period of 1911 to 1949 Xi'an gradually became less isolated from the outer world. Before the revolution the city had already established its first telegraph office (in 1885) and international post office (in 1902). The railway did not reach Xi'an until 1934, but Westerners started to visit the city in increasing numbers from the turn of the century onwards, usually making contact with the China Inland Mission, the Scandinavian Alliance Mission or the English Baptists, all of whom were represented in the city. They returned, frequently to write books, informing (and often misinforming) the outside world about 'ancient Sian-fu':

> It will be long before the City of Western Peace becomes the resort of sightseers. Yet Sian and its neighbourhood provide more sights to see than most inland Chinese capitals, in case the blessed day of trains de luxe and steam-heated hotels should ever draw for it. The rolling plain, all round as far as you can see, is full of mounds and barrows; and two noble pagodas invite inspection. Or you can mount the wall and study the whole flat extent of the city; you can ascend the Drum Tower, and from the vast darkness of its loft look out towards the turquoise roofs of the Mahometan mosque, and, beyond these, to the orange gables of the Imperial Palace, where the Grand Dowager pitched her flying tents in 1900.
>
> (From *On the Eaves of the World* by Reginald Farrar, 1917)

During the struggle for power in the 1920s and '30s, Xi'an was of some strategic importance and once again in its history played a dramatic role: in 1926, it was occupied by a pro-Nationalist Shaanxi general, Yang Hucheng, and was promptly surrounded by an anti-Nationalist force. So began the six-month Siege of Xi'an. When it was finally lifted, some 50,000 were said to have died. Revolution Park marks the place where they were buried (see page 128).

In the struggle between communist and Nationalist forces, Xi'an came to the forefront in 1936, when Huaqing Hot Springs was the scene of the so-called Xi'an Incident (see page 104). Chiang Kai-shek, intent on getting rid of domestic communist opposition before putting up resistance to the invading Japanese, was arrested by two Nationalist generals, Yang Hucheng and the leader of the displaced Northeastern Army, Zhang Xueliang, and forced to agree to join the communists against the common enemy, the Japanese. Xi'an became a vital link between the communist headquarters in Yan'an and the outside world through the establishment of the Eighth Route Army Office (see page 128).

During the Sino-Japanese War, Xi'an was bombed, but never occupied by the Japanese. After the war, the city was controlled by Nationalist troops until it was taken by communist forces on 20 May 1949. The People's Republic of China was inaugurated less than five months later.

XI'AN UNDER THE PEOPLE'S REPUBLIC

Xi'an has grown much larger in the past 40 years, both in size and population. Many new industries have also been established. The initial impetus for this growth came from the Government whose policy was to give priority to the development of the cities in the interior.

In 1949 Xi'an did not extend much further than the walled city, covering only 13.2 square kilometres (5 square miles). Today the city has spread to 100 square kilometres (38.5 square miles), an extent even larger than the Tang capital of Chang'an which occupied an area of 81 square kilometres (31.2 square miles) within the outer walls. The modern city is not so regular in its layout as its great predecessor, and it extends further to the east and west than the Tang city.

The population has increased rapidly since the 1930s when it was between 200,000 and 300,000. Today it is 3.4 million, although this includes the people living within the jurisdiction of the city. The urban population numbers around 2 million.

If you want to see something of the city's recent industrial and social development, CITS can arrange visits to model factories, hospitals, schools, district neighbourhoods and farming communities, although these are no longer included as a matter of course on tour itineraries.

Sights

SHAANXI MUSEUM

The Shaanxi Museum was formally established in 1952 and occupies the former Temple of Confucius along the inside of the southern section of the city wall, on Baishulin Jie. It used to be the principal museum for Shaanxi and displayed antiquities brought from every part of the province. It is particularly famous for its Forest of Steles, but the 2,600-odd exhibits shown in chronological order to illustrate the history of Shaanxi have now been transferred to the new Shaanxi History Museum (see page 112) which opened in July 1991. The halls vacated are now used to display temporary exhibitions.

The museum is open from 8.30 am to 6 pm, and tickets are sold up to 5 pm.

■ THE FOREST OF STELES (BEILIN)

This famous collection of over 1,000 inscribed stones began in 1090 when a large Confucian collection of steles cut in AD 837—the oldest existing texts of the Confucian classics—was moved for safekeeping to the back of the Temple of Confucius. The collection slowly grew until by the 18th century it was already called by its present name, the Forest of Steles. It is the largest collection of its kind in China. This stone library is part of the Shaanxi Museum.

The art of inscribing on stone began in China at least as early as the fourth century BC. The earliest examples that have survived from this time are the ten Stone Drums of Qin. Recording a hunting party led by a Duke of Qin, they were discovered during the Tang Dynasty at Fengxiang, about 145 kilometres (90 miles) west of Xi'an. The originals are now in Beijing but a reproduction of one of them is on display in the Shaanxi History Museum (see page 112).

From the Han Dynasty onwards flat stones were cut with either text or pictures, not only for commemorative purposes but also to make it possible to reproduce them on paper by taking rubbings. These rubbings, made into either scrolls or books, often serve as models for calligraphy practice.

Unfortunately, all explanatory notes for the collection are in Chinese so unless you have a competent guide-interpreter you may well leave impressed but mystified by these grey-black slabs of stone.

As a rough guide, the contents of the Forest of Steles can be divided into four groups: works of literature and philosophy, historical records, calligraphy and pictorial stones. Of most immediate interest are the pictorial stones in Room Four, which are displayed with some stones engraved with historical records. They are almost all relatively late, from the Ming (1368–1644) or Qing (1644–1911). As well as landscapes and portraits—notably of Confucius and Bodhidarma—there are some fascinating stones with allegorical pictures and some texts written to appear like pictures (it was a Qing fashion to create pictures composed of Chinese characters). Room Three houses the calligraphy collection which is of great importance. There are two

Portrait of Confucius on a tablet, the Forest of Steles

reconstructed examples of the calligraphy of Wang Xizhi (AD 321–379) which have had immense influence on the art of the brush, together with pieces by many of the Tang-dynasty masters.

If you would like to see the famous Nestorian Stele, cut in 781, it is in Room Two, immediately to the left of the entrance. It records the history of the Nestorian Christian community in Chang'an from its founding in the seventh century by a Syrian missionary. Room One contains the nucleus of the collection, the set of 114 stones engraved in AD 837 with the definitive text of the Confucian classics. Inscribed on both sides of the stones, the text uses a staggering total of 650,252 characters.

Room Five exhibits stone tablets of Song, Yuan, Ming and Qing dynasties. They are mainly concerned with temple renovation and records of merit. In Room Six most of the inscriptions are poetic, inscribed by the literati of the Qing. Emperors, noted ministers and famous calligraphers of various dynasties have left many inscriptions, examples of which are displayed in Room Seven.

■ THE STONE SCULPTURE GALLERY

This gallery, which is beside the Forest of Steles, has a collection of about 70 sculptures and relief carving of unrivalled quality. However, not all of the stones are originals (in particular the horse from the tomb of 'Swift Cavalry General' Huo Qubing is a reproduction). The most famous exhibits are the six bas-reliefs, four of them original, from the Zhao Ling, the Mausoleum of Emperor Tang Taizong (see page 85). There are also a number of large animals which once lined the approaches to imperial tombs of the Han and Tang. At the end of the gallery are some Buddhist statues including a very beautiful torso of a bodhisattva, showing strong Indian influence, and a Avalokitesvara on an elaborate lotus throne. Both are from the Tang period.

SHAANXI HISTORY MUSEUM

The National Museum of Shaanxi History opened in 1991, eighteen years after Premier Zhou Enlai first suggested that such an establishment was needed to exhibit the province's archaeological treasures. Occupying a large site in Xi'an's southern suburbs close to the Big Goose Pagoda, the museum, housed in a complex of striking Tang-dynasty style pavilions, is an absolute must for every visitor to the city.

The exhibits here represent the very best of the museum's collection, the greater portion of which remain stored in its underground warehouse. The permanent exhibition on the ground and first floors is supplemented by touring exhibitions—usually two—in the basement. Included elsewhere in the palatial-style buildings are lecture theatres, conference rooms, a library, research laboratories and an extensive restoration centre. A new unit for restoration was recently funded by an Italian Antiquities

Department donation of US$4 million.

For security reasons, visitors to the museum must leave their bags in the cloak-room before entering the galleries.

A spacious entrance hall greets visitors with its reproduction lion from Qian Ling (see page 73). Pace yourself on this stunning marathon walk through a million years of Chinese history. You need at least three hours in this museum. For longer-stay visitors to Xi'an, a return visit after trips to outlying sites may help to put the sights they have seen into context.

The exhibits on the ground and first floors are arranged in chronological dynastic order.

■ PREHISTORY TO 2000 BC

At the entrance to the first gallery a relief map of Shaanxi Province shows the three main landscape divisions of the province, from north to south: the loess lands of the Yellow Earth Plateau, the Guanzhong Plain around the Wei River and the Qinling mountains. Most of the exhibits in this museum were unearthed from the Guan-zhong Plain, the cradle of Chinese civilization. Relics in this room hail from Shaanxi's three main prehistoric sites—Lantian, Dali and Banpo. Fossilized remains of old Stone-Age man were discovered at Lantian and Dali, while at Banpo the foundations of a Neolithic village have been excavated (see page 39). Pottery with distinctive markings were among the most remarkable finds at Banpo.

■ XIA, SHANG, WESTERN AND EASTERN ZHOU DYNASTIES

The second gallery covers the 21st century BC to 770 BC, the dawn of the iron and bronze ages. By the Shang and Zhou dynasties, metalworking techniques had become highly sophisticated. Bronze was used in weapons for hunting as well as in battle, ritual implements, agricultural tools, and household and palace utensils. Particularly striking are the handsome cooking tripods called *ding*, some up to one metre (3.3 feet) in height. Elegant bulbous-based and thin-legged wine vessels called *jue* were used for warming liquor. Weapons include daggers, halberds and spear-heads, as well as sickle-shaped scabbards with sawtooth edges.

Moving onto the relics from the Western Zhou and later the Eastern Zhou, one sees the same material, bronze, cast into more elegant, beautiful and practical wares. Extremely impressive are the bronze bells. There is a single Shicheng Bell, about the size of the largest of watermelons, a musical instrument used in the home of a noble-man or even at court. In a separate display case close-by is one of the museum's finest pieces, a set of chime bells (*bianzhong*). The set consists of eight bells suspended from a wooden beam and arranged according to size. Strangely enough, although their number corresponds to the eight notes of an octave, the fourth and seventh

Village life—houses dug out of loess embankments can be seen in the Xi'an countryside

notes, *fa* and *ti*, are absent. Discovered at Fufeng County, the bells were almost certainly used to entertain the courts established by the Zhou (see page 40).

Other examples of aesthetic refinement in Zhou bronzeware include a fine ox-shaped wine vessel, an ornate incense burner and an artist's palette.

■ SPRING AND AUTUMN PERIOD, THE WARRING STATES AND QIN DYNASTY
770 BC–206 BC

In the third gallery the exhibits highlight progress made during the Qin Dynasty in the fields of construction, plumbing, metallurgy, agriculture and irrigation, weaponry and public works. However, rapid economic and technical development had already begun to take place in the pre-imperial period. Around 400 BC, the casting of iron became widespread, as evidenced by the many remains of axes, spades and swords excavated in Shaanxi, a region rich in minerals.

The most important relics from Qin times are, of course, the terracotta warriors (four of which are on display here), but visitors are sure to go to the museum built at the excavations (see page 48). Look instead for a tiger tally. This ingenious object was a symbol of imperial authority—its holder or recipient could be certain orders were genuine if both halves of the tally matched. Although not immediately apparent, the tally comes in two symmetrical parts split along the animal's backbone.

■ HAN DYNASTY 202 BC–AD 220

An elaborate wooden map on the wall in this exhibition room, the first one upstairs on the left, highlights the expansion of Han China. The Silk Road became important during this period (see page 57). Travellers who have visited the Han tombs north of Xi'an will see fine examples of funerary objects, such as a gold incense burner discovered at the tomb of the Han general, Huo Qubing (see page 61). Other excavated tombs in the north Guanzhong Plain have yielded tomb figurines which were on a more modest scale than Qin Shihuangdi's terracotta army, but which nevertheless provide much information about daily life at that time.

To keep the deceased content in the afterlife a variety of models in pottery were produced, including water wells, pigsties, barns and domestic animals such as oxen, chicken and dogs. For those who cannot get to Xianyang Museum, a couple of hundred of the miniature terracotta army are shown here (see page 63).

Finally, there are a number of exhibits to illustrate Han ingenuity. Paper making, one of the four great Chinese inventions—the others were gunpowder, printing and the compass—is generally attributed to the Han Wudi period of 140–87 BC. This early paper was produced from hemp fibre mixed with ramie by a process of pulping, boiling and drying. Another material unique to China was silk. A third group of relics includes gear cogs, nuts and hinges.

■ WEI, JIN, NORTHERN AND SOUTHERN DYNASTIES AD 220–581

A small room is devoted to the relics of this period, during which Chang'an lost its capital status and remained relatively unimportant until it regained its pre-eminence as a centre of imperial power and cultural influence under the Tang rulers.

■ SUI AND TANG DYNASTY AD 581–907.

This was a period that corresponds to Xi'an's restoration as the unified empire's capital. In particular, the brilliance of the mid-Tang period is reflected in the most extensive and spectacular collection of exhibits in this museum. A wooden map, similar to the one in the Han gallery, shows the expansion of Tang China, which capitalized on Sui unification and encompassed present-day Mongolia, Vietnam and parts of Kazakhstan as well as what we recognize as the People's Republic of China today. Beyond, one is confronted by display cases full of markedly colourful relics, consisting in the main of tri-coloured glazed pottery articles. Foremost amongst these are the handsome horses and camels, both one- and two-humped species, which bear witness to Chang'an's links to foreign lands by means of the Silk Road. Other figures include heavenly gods stamping on evil and ugly aliens; gargoyle-like animals which were used as guardians of tombs; and Tang beauties with chubby cheeks and bouffant hairstyles, shod in shoes with upturned toes. The vanity of Tang women is highlighted by the mirrors on display. These are of highly polished metal, but it is their ornately decorated backs that are of particular interest.

As a backdrop to these colourful relics, some murals removed from tomb passageways and chambers are displayed. The themes illustrated relate to recreation, fashion and court activities. Most striking are murals showing polo-playing, hunting, ladies being attended by maidservants and court officials receiving foreign guests.

■ SONG, YUAN, MING AND QING DYNASTIES

Chang'an was eclipsed with the collapse of the Tang in the early tenth century and neither Xi'an nor its environs ever dominated national affairs again. Although spanning a millennium, the relics from this period only occupy a small area. Particularly noteworthy, however, are the fine porcelain pieces, characteristically sea-green or ivory in colour, some examples of which were produced by the *dingyao* kilns during the Song Dynasty. Another striking display relates to the Ming—an array of 300 colourfully painted miniature pottery figures unearthed at the tomb of a Shaanxi official.

Transparencies, postcards and historical books are sold at counters in the foyer. In the basement, on the west side, a showroom has an extensive selection of reproduction relics.

THE BELL TOWER

Each Ming city had a bell tower and a drum tower. The bell was sounded at dawn and the drum at dusk. The two buildings still exist in many Chinese cities, but those at Xi'an are the best known in China.

The Bell Tower was originally built in 1384 at the intersection of Xi Dajie and Guangji Jie. This was the centre of the site of the old Tang Imperial City, where the government offices had been located. The tower was removed in 1582 and rebuilt in its present position in the centre of the southern section of the walled city, overlooking the four avenues which lead to the four gates. It was restored in 1739. Now seemingly enmeshed in overhead trolley bus wires, it is nevertheless proudly regarded as the symbol of the city's centre.

The Bell Tower is set on a square brick platform, each side of which is 35.5 metres (116 feet) long, with an arched gateway at ground level. The platform is 8.6 metres (28 feet) high and on top is a triple-eaved, two-storey wooden structure, a further 27.4 metres (90 feet) high. There is a fine view in all directions from the parapet on the second floor. The inside is remarkable as an example of the very intri-

Reconstructed Ming-dynasty city walls and moat

cate roof truss system used in Ming and Qing wooden architecture. The original great bell no longer exists, but a small Ming-period bell is kept in a corner of the brick platform.

The Bell Tower is open from 9.10 am to 5.30 pm.

THE DRUM TOWER

The Drum Tower is quite similar to the nearby Bell Tower, except for its rectangular shape. It was first built in 1380, and restored in 1669, 1739 and 1953. The brick base, on which the wooden structure is built, is 52.6 metres (172 feet) long, 38 metres (125 feet) wide and 7.7 metres (25 feet) high. A road goes straight through it, under a vaulted archway. The triple-roofed, two-storey wooden building is a further 25.3 metres (83 feet) high off its brick platform. The second storey, which is surrounded by a parapet, is now used as an antique shop, for which it provides a very original setting. The immediate surroundings are more interesting than those of the Bell Tower. Less encumbered by wires, the Drum Tower looks down on the irregular grey-tiled roofs of the Muslim quarter.

The Drum Tower is open from 8.30 am to 5.30 pm and is two blocks west of the Bell Tower.

Song-dynasty celadon pot

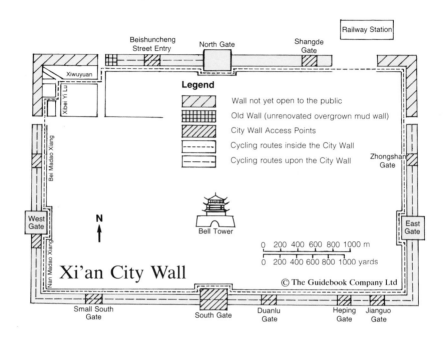

Xi'an City Wall

© The Guidebook Company Ltd

THE MING CITY WALL AND GATES

Xi'an's 14th-century wall still stands, although today it is intersected by a few modern roads. It is one of the most important city walls in China and certainly one of the best examples from the Ming.

The circumference is 13.7 kilometres (8.5 miles), and it is 12 metres (40 feet) high, 12–14 metres (40–46 feet) wide at the top and 15–18 metres (49–59 feet) wide at the bottom. It is surrounded by a moat.

The Ming city gates face the four cardinal points, set off-centre in each of the sides of the rectangular wall. Originally each gate had two structures: the gate tower, a triple-eaved building 34.6 metres (114 feet) long, and beyond, on the city wall itself, was the massive archers' tower, 53.2 metres (175 feet) in length, with 48 openings on the outer face from which missiles could be fired on a potential enemy. The towers above the South Gate, to which visitors are usually taken, are well preserved; but instead of guardrooms and barracks you will now find inside them souvenir shops and showrooms.

The West Gate has recently been opened to the public. There is an antiques exhibition inside the gate tower.

The city wall, although rebuilt, does not yet make up an unbroken rectangle. It is best regarded as a series of cul-de-sacs. The longest unbroken section is from the West Gate to the East Gate, a distance of approximately five kilometres (three miles). Cycling on top of the wall in this section is peaceful, less dangerous and somewhat cleaner than in the streets below. Moreover, it gives you a bird's eye view of the city itself.

The wall can also be followed by cycling inside the structure along a route which, for the most part, is a narrow, quiet lane, traffic-free apart from bicycles, of course.

There are ten stairways to the top of the wall. Landscaping of the area between the wall and moat has provided a pleasant setting for a stroll. Restoration work on three gates is complete .

THE GREAT MOSQUE

The beautiful mosque lies close to the Drum Tower in Huajue Xiang. It is surrounded by the old houses and narrow lanes of Xi'an's Muslim, or Hui, community. The mosque is still active: on ordinary days about 100 men pray there, with perhaps 1,000 on Fridays. Of the ten or so functioning mosques in the city this is the only one which is open to visitors, although non-Muslims are not admitted at prayer times.

Islam has been the most enduring of all faiths in Xi'an. It was first introduced by Arab merchants during the Tang Dynasty, and flourished during the Yuan (1279–1368). The Muslims gradually became concentrated in the northwestern part of the walled city, where they remain to this day. The community now numbers about 50,000. There were said to be 14 mosques open before the Cultural Revolution put a stop to Muslim privileges. But today, the community is regaining its lost ground. It has its own primary school, food shops and restaurants (these are popular with the Han Chinese as well). Although the Muslims generally work on Fridays, they do observe Ramadan, the month of fasting from sunrise to sunset. They can often be distinguished from the Han Chinese by their white caps and long beards.

The Great Mosque survived the Cultural Revolution virtually unscathed and remains an outstanding Chinese re-interpretation of an Islamic place of worship. It was founded in AD 742, according to a stone tablet in the mosque, but nothing from this Tang period survives. The present layout dates from the 14th century. Restoration work was done in 1527, 1606 and 1768. The mosque occupies a rectangle 250 metres by 47 metres (820 feet by 155 feet), divided into four courtyards. Throughout there are walls with decoratively carved brick reliefs and the buildings are roofed with beautiful turquoise tiles.

Chimera

To this Tang capital, already old in refinement, Arabs and Persians arrived by the Silk Route or the southern ports. They came as merchants and mercenary soldiers, and the houses of their Muslim descendants, who call themselve Hui, still cluster in whitewashed lanes. Yet the people looked identical to Han Chinese, and when I ventured into the chief mosque I was surrounded by pagodas, dragon-screens and tilted eaves. Only when I looked closer did I notice that on some memorials Chinese characters gave way to the dotted swing of Arabic, and the prayer-hall enclosed no plump idol but an empty space, inviting a god only in the mind.

Outside, a few caretakers were sweeping leaves along the garden pathways. The chanting of the Koran sounded from a closed room. In one arcade an old man, the skin peeled white about his eyes, was singing in a high, weak voice, while a quorum of ancients seated round him quavered applause. Amongst them the imam of the mosque—a dark, lordly figure— exuded urbane authority. I sidled into talk with him. I was intrigued, I said, by the provenance of his people.

'We arrived in Xi'an as simple traders', he said, 'and nobody has any record of his ancestry except in his head. Our people came along the Silk Road during the Tang years.' His fingers made a little galloping motion in the air. 'But we stopped speaking Arabic long ago. Even I can only read the classical language of the Koran.'

'But you've been to Mecca?'

'I made the pilgrimage in 1956.'

He was dressed portentously in white cap and blue-grey robes. I played with the idea of his Arab-Persian descent for a while, studying his hirsute chin and tufted eyebrows. But nothing in his face—nor in that of anyone else—betrayed a trace of western Asia. 'You all look Chinese,' I said.

'Yes,' he answered bluntly. 'I can't tell any difference myself, not in any of us—and there are fifty thousand Hui in the city. But I suppose if we hadn't intermarried we would have died out. Still, it's a mystery.'

'In the Cultural Revolution . . . . '

'Oh that.' He smoothed his hands resolutely over his robes. 'The Red

Guards arrived planning to smash up the mosque, but I sat them down and talked to them. I told them this was a historical place of great importance. Then . . . .'—even now he looked surprised by the outcome—'then they just left. They simply went away.' A flicker of his fingers dispelled them. 'The mosque was closed down, of course, and we went into the fields . . . . But nobody touched it.'

A lesser man would have called it a miracle.

Colin Thubron, Behind the Wall

Xi'an Muslims at prayer

The first courtyard, which was restored in 1981, has an elaborate wooden arch nine metres (29.5 feet) high dating from the 17th century. Most visitors enter the mosque through a gate leading into the second courtyard. This contains a stone arch and two free-standing steles. One bears the calligraphy of a famous Song master, Mi Fu (1051–1107), the other that of Dong Qichang of the Ming.

At the entrance to the third courtyard is a Stele Hall with tablets of the Ming and Qing periods inscribed in Chinese, Arabic and Persian. The Stele of the Months, written in Arabic by an imam in 1733, bears information about the Islamic calendar.

In the middle of the third courtyard is the minaret, an octagonal pagoda with a triple roof of turquoise tiles, known as the Shengxin Tower. On either side are sets of rooms. In one section, next to the imam's living quarters, there is a fascinating Qing-dynasty map of the Islamic world painted by Chinese Muslims with the black cube of the Kaaba at Mecca in the centre. In the same room is kept an illuminated, hand-written Koran dating from the Qing Dynasty.

The fourth courtyard, the principal one of the complex, contains the Prayer Hall. By the entrance is a small room with an upright stele recording in Chinese the foundation of the mosque in AD 742. The stone itself is probably not original. In front of the entrance is the ornamental Phoenix Pavilion with a board proclaiming the 'One Truth of the One God', written during the Ming. Behind the Phoenix Pavilion are two fountains flanked by two small stele pavilions and behind them is the broad, raised stone terrace used for worship.

The large Prayer Hall dates from the Ming; the board outside the main door was bestowed by the Yongle Emperor (reigned 1403–24). The ornate woodwork inside is mainly of this period. There is a coffered ceiling, each panel containing different Arabic inscriptions. The mihrab at the far end has some fine carving.

To walk to the Great Mosque go north along the street that passes under the Drum Tower, and take the first left. A sign in English indicates the way. It is open from 8.30 am to 6 pm.

THE TEMPLE OF THE EIGHT IMMORTALS

China's indigenous religion, Daoism (Taoism), is best represented in Xi'an by the Temple of the Eight Immortals (Baxian An).

Located just east of the city wall, it housed 100 priests as recently as 20 years ago. But at the start of the Cultural Revolution in 1966 half the buildings were demolished by iconoclastic Red Guards, and those that survived were converted into a machine plant. Under a decade-long restoration programme initiated in 1981, the plant has now been moved out and the temple halls rebuilt and redecorated. A part of the temple grounds is to be landscaped as a garden.

The temple is now functioning again as a place of worship and a centre for the training of priests. There are now more than 30 of them, easily distinguishable from other Chinese by their long hair, usually plaited and stuffed into one of nine different types of black hat according to their sect, sage-like long beards, white shirts, blue smocks, white gaiters and black canvas shoes.

Although no foundation stele exists, it is thought the temple was established during the Northern Song (AD 960–1127). It expanded during the Yuan and Ming, and became particularly important during the Qing. When the imperial court was in exile in Xi'an (1900–01), the Empresss Dowager Cixi grew especially fond of the temple and used to go there to paint peonies.

A cultural shopping street will be opened in the temple precincts opposite the main gate of the complex. There are also a few shops within the temple grounds themselves. The reforms sweeping China have reached the Daoists too. Traditionally the Daoist priests occupied themselves with a minimum of secular chores, save for those necessary to meet primary needs. Now they are more economically minded as they let shops to artists and craftsmen and manage a *zhaodaisuo*—a hostel at present not open to foreign guests.

To get to the Temple of Eight Immortals by public transport, take trolley bus number 104, alighting at the first stop outside the wall. Walk back along Changle Lu and take the first left. When the road ends, bear right and then left. The temple compound is on the right. Drivers and neighbourhood people can direct you.

EASTERN PEAK TEMPLE

This Daoist complex, founded in 1116, is situated about 50 metres (55 yards) from the northwest corner of the East Gate. It is now in the grounds of a primary school and normally closed but the inquisitive visitor can sometimes persuade the caretaker to open the building for a brief look. The temple was dedicated to the cult of Tai Shan, the most important of the sacred mountains of China. Today, though all the altars have of course gone, there are still a few traces of the once-famous frescoes. A small Qing pavilion at the rear of the compound, in bad condition, has additional murals.

To walk to the temple from the East Gate, just look for the blue, lacquered roof and follow the small alleyway that leads you there.

THE TEMPLE OF THE TOWN GOD

Within walking distance of the Bell Tower, this temple is now a school and warehouse but some of the buildings are still in reasonable condition and are expected to be renovated shortly. It is believed that the Government will arrange to give the temple a complete facelift. The temple dates back to 1389, but was moved to its present site in 1432. It has been rebuilt and restored many times since, notably in 1723 when materials were utilized from the 14th-century palace of the Prince of Qin, Zhu Shuang. The main hall, built in 1723, survives with ornate carved doors. In front

Lost Luggage in Sianfu

In June 1936, the American correspondent Edgar Snow left the peaceful campus of Yanjing University in Beijing, where he had been teaching in the school of journalism, to travel to the war-torn hinterland of China on his toughest mission to date. Five years previously the Japanese had annexed Manchuria. Further incursions by the Japanese went unchecked as civil war between Nationalists and communists kept the armies occupied. Just eight months before, Mao Zedong had led the communist retreat—later called the Long March—from soviet areas in the southeastern province of Jiangxi to a new base in northern Shaanxi. Edgar Snow wanted to find the Red Bandits, as the communists were called, interview their leader Mao, and report their manifesto for China to the world.

Inoculated against smallpox, cholera, typhus, plague and typhoid and armed with a letter written in invisible ink testifying his credentials as a trustworthy journalist, Snow boarded the night train to Zhengzhou where he would change for Sianfu (Xi'an). Later he disclosed that the introduction was written by Soong Chingling (Song Qingling), widow of Sun Yat-sen.

Sianfu—Prefecture of Western Peace—was the headquarters of two warlords and their own troops: General Yang Hucheng and Marshall Zhang Xueliang. Both were poised to implement what Generalissimo Chiang Kai-shek hoped would be the final suppression of the Red Bandits in the north.

On arrival at Sianfu's 'new and handsome railway station', Edgar Snow took a room, as he had been instructed, in the Xijing Hotel on the west side of present-day Jiefang Lu (the building now houses the Provincial Travel Bureau). There he waited patiently for a man who would identify himself as 'Wang'. A few days later, a pastor of that name, fluent in English thanks to his missionary education in Shanghai, came to the hotel. He was to be the go-between responsible for arranging Snow's onward travel to the communists' capital of Bao'an, 350 kilometres (215 miles) away in the north.

A few days later Snow, escorted by troops from Zhang Xueliang's army, passed through the high wooden gates of the walled city in the half light of dawn. After crossing the Wei River by ferry and passing through a strip of no man's land, he reached Red territory. From a village within this territory, where he met Zhou Enlai, he was escorted at last into the presence of the communist leader.

What happened in the ensuing few months is journalistic history. Snow interviewed Mao Zedong over many nights, taking notes which in the end totalled about 20,000 words. From these and talks with other leaders Snow was able to write the first authentic account of the life and conditions of the northwestern communist enclave, the revolutionary struggles of Mao and his comrades, and the fundamental policies of the People's Soviet Republic.

In mid-October 1936, Snow bid farewell to his communist hosts, and about a week later crossed safely behind Nationalist lines again. He rode on to a town where a truck waited to take him back to Sianfu. As he prepared to disembark near the Drum Tower, he asked one of his escorts to toss down his kitbag. To his horror, it could not be found. In the bag were a dozen diaries and notebooks, 30 rolls of film and many magazines, newspapers and documents he had collected during his time in Red territory. It then dawned on the travellers that Snow's bag had been stuffed into a gunnysack amongst broken rifles and guns, which had been offloaded at Xianyang 30 kilometres (18 miles) back.

The truck driver proposed they waited till the next day to retrieve the bag, but Snow insisted on the search being made without delay. The driver returned to Xianyang and the precious bag was recovered. Snow's sense of urgency proved justified. The next day much of Sianfu was cordoned off and traffic was cleared from the roads, for Chiang Kai-shek had decided to pay a sudden call on the city.

The manuscript of *Red Star over China* was completed within an astonishing eight months in Beijing, where Snow returned to live. The 500-page epic was first published in England in 1937 and has since become a classic.

In Xi'an, Edgar Snow's contribution to the world's understanding of Chinese communism is remembered by the Snow Studies Centre, based at the Eighth Route Army Office Museum. The centre was established in February 1992, the 20th anniversary of Snow's death. Many of the journalist's belongings, including his khaki uniform, knapsack and grass sandals, were donated to the centre by his family.

of it there is an elaborate wooden arch in good condition.

A building to the south which used to be a theatre is currently an office. A wooden arch formerly comprised the gate of the temple, but was demolished during the Cultural Revolution.

To get to the Temple of the Town God, walk along Xi Dajie to building number 257, then take the small lane running north through a small goods market called Town God Temple Market (Chenghuang Miao). The temple is at the end of the market.

REVOLUTION PARK

Revolution Park (Geming Gongyuan), in the northwest of the walled city, is where those who died in the 1926 Siege of Xi'an are buried. Anti-Nationalist forces laid siege to Xi'an on 15 May 1926 after the city had been occupied by a pro-Nationalist general, Yang Hucheng. Despite appalling starvation and a fierce bombing attack, the city held out until 28 November 1926, when the siege was finally lifted. Yang Hucheng wrote the funeral couplet for those 50,000 inhabitants and refugees who are said to have died during the siege:

> They led glorious lives and died a glorious death.
> Their merits are known throughout Shaanxi, as are their regrets.

The park contains a three-storeyed pagoda erected in 1927. As the largest park within the city walls, it is very popular with the local townspeople and especially crowded on Sundays.

THE EIGHTH ROUTE ARMY OFFICE MUSEUM

Near Revolution Park at 1 Qixianzhuang, just off Beixin Jie, is the Eighth Route Army Office (initially called the Red Army Liaison Office) which is now a museum. It was founded immediately after the Xi'an Incident which had resulted in the Nationalists and communists joining forces against the Japanese (see page 104).

The office once linked the headquarters of the Communist Party in Yan'an in northern Shaanxi with the outside world in the struggle against the Japanese. It obtained vital supplies for Yan'an, helped recruits make their way there, and publicized the polices of the party leadership. The office functioned until July 1947. It is now preserved as it was during the Sino-Japanese War.

Occupying a series of plain, but attractive, grey and white one-storey buildings set around four courtyards, the museum is a good deal more interesting than its name might suggest. There is an exhibition room with many fascinating photographs taken in Shaanxi during the 1930s and '40s. Visitors are also shown the rooms where important communist leaders, including Zhou Enlai and Deng Xiaoping, stayed. The Canadian doctor Norman Bethune, later to become almost a cult figure in China, was also once a visitor here. The museum houses the Snow Studies Centre (see page 126), which was opened in 1992.

The office still has its 1939 Chevrolet, originally imported from Hong Kong and used for urgent missions to Yan'an. The radio room contains the old transmitter and receiver. Even the director of the museum is an interesting character: Tang Bin, a veteran soldier, joined the Communist Fourth Route Army in Sichuan in 1933, when he was only 16, and eventually became a guard in the Eighth Route Army Office in Lanzhou from 1938 to 1946, later rising to a company commander in the air force. He has been the director of the museum since 1964.

The museum is open 9 am to 5 pm.

QIN PALACE

This reproduction Qin Palace, east of the Big Goose Pagoda, was built in 1988 for the IMAX film *Qin Shihuang*, a joint-venture production between Xi'an Film Studio and the Canadian State Film Bureau.

A large dusty concourse in front of the elevated palace façade is dotted with a hotch-potch of redundant film-set props—tanks, artillery pieces, concrete horses and chariots—which seem a great hit with the Chinese who flock here on outings with their children.

According to legend, the First Emperor, Qin Shihuangdi, used the weapons he confiscated to make 12 monolithic copper statues. Replicas of these stand sentinel on the avenue approach to the palace. Climbing up the long flight of steps you reach the only hall of the palace, where dummies are dressed in Qin costume. On the right-hand side of the hall is an exhibition room displaying stills of Xi'an Film Studio's most successful movies, notably *Life*, *Red Sorghum* and more recently *After the Final Battle*, a look at the re-education of Kuomintang officers in the post-Liberation years of the People's Republic.

At ground level on the left is an underground *Pilgrimage to the West* (admission extra). Walking through this labyrinth of dark passages you see illuminated models of the novel's characters and hear sound effects en route to 'The Kingdoms Beyond the Himalayas'.

All film studios appear fake and shoddy when seen close up, and this one is no exception.

To get to the Qin Palace take bus number 5 and alight at Dayan Ta (the Big Goose Pagoda). Walk towards the pagoda. At the fork junction bear left and continue straight on for about 400 metres (about 440 yards).

The Qin Palace is open from 8.30 am to 6.30 pm. Last tickets are sold at 5.30 pm.

Ceremonial dragon dance (above); traditional gong and drum ensemble (below),
at the World Travel Day outside the Qin Palace

Recommended Reading

History and Religion

K Ch'en: *Buddhism in China, A Historical Survey* (Princeton University Press, Princetown, New Jersey, 1964)

J Bertram: *First Act in China: The Story of the Sian Mutiny* (1938, reprinted by Hyperion Press, Westport, Conn, 1973)

M Zanchen (translated by Wang Zhao): *The Life of General Yang Hucheng* (Joint Publishing Company, Hong Kong, 1981)

E Reischauer: *Ennin's Diary* (Ronald Press Company, New York, 1955)

Peter Hopkirk: *Foreign Devils on the Silk Road* (Oxford University Press reprint, 1986)

Edgar Snow: *Red Star Over China* (Random House, USA, 1938)

Arts and Archaeology

W Watson: *Ancient China, The Discoveries of Post-Liberation Archaeology* (BBC, London, 1974)

B Laufer: *Chinese Pottery of the Han Dynasty* (1909, reprinted by Charles E Tuttle, Vermont and Tokyo, 1962)

A Wonder of the World Treasures of the Nation: Terra-Cotta Army of Emperor Qin Shihuang (Shaanxi Travel & Tourism Publishing House, 1990)

Xi'an: World Ancient Chinese Capital for over a Thousand Years (Shaanxi People's Fine Arts Publishing House, 1990)

Li Hui: *Xi'an: The Famous Ancient Capital of China* (Shaanxi Tourism Bureau, 1990)

Literature

Arthur Cooper: *Li Po and Tu Fu* (Penguin Books, Harmondsworth, 1979)

Y Inoue (translated by J T Araki and E Seidensticker): *Lou-lan and Other Stories* (Kodansha International Limited, New York and San Francisco, 1979)

E R Hughes: *Two Chinese Poets, Vignettes of Han Life and Thought* (Princeton University Press, Princeton, New Jersey, 1960)

Arthur Waley: *The Life and Times of Po Chü-i 772–846* (George Allen & Unwin, London, 1949)

Translated by Yang Xianyi and Gladys Yang: *Poetry and Prose of the Tang and Song* (Panda Books, Beijing, 1984)

Twentieth-century Travellers

Violet Cressy-Marcks: *Journey into China* (Hodder and Stoughton, London, 1940)

S Eliasson (translated by K John): *Dragon Wang's River* (Methuen and Company Limited, London, 1957)

R Farrar: *On the Eaves of the World* (E Arnold, London, 1917)

Peter Fleming: *News From Tartary* (1936, reprinted by Futura Publications, London, 1980)

F H Nichols: *Through Hidden Shensi* (Charles Scribner's Sons, New York, 1902)

R Stirling Clark and A de C Sowerby: *Through Shen-Kan: The Account of the Clark Expedition in North China 1908–09* (T Fisher Unwin, London, 1912)

Lynn Pan: *China's Sorrow—Journeys Around the Yellow River* (Century, London, 1985)

William Lindesay: *Alone on the Great Wall* (Hodder & Stoughton, London, 1989 and Fulcrum Publishing, Colorado, USA, 1991)

A Chronology of Periods in Chinese History

Palaeolithic	c.600,000–7000BC
Neolithic	c.7000–1600 BC
Shang	c.1600–1027 BC
Western Zhou	1027–771 BC
Eastern Zhou	770–256 BC
Spring and Autumn Annals	770–476 BC
Warring States	475–221 BC
Qin	221–206 BC
Western (Former) Han	206BC–8 AD
Xin	9–24
Eastern (Later) Han	25–220
Three Kingdoms	220–265
Western Jin	265–316
Northern and Southern Dynasties	317–589
Sixteen Kingdoms	317–439
Former Zhao	304–329
Former Qin	351–383
Later Qin	384–417
Northern Wei	386–534
Western Wei	535–556
Northern Zhou	557–581
Sui	581–618
Tang	618–907
Five Dynasties	907–960
Northern Song	960–1127
Southern Song	1127–1279
Jin (Jurchen)	1115–1234
Yuan (Mongol)	1279–1368
Ming	1368–1644
Qing (Manchu)	1644–1911
Republic of China	1911–1949
People's Republic of China	1949–

A Guide to Pronouncing Chinese Names

The official system of Romanization used in China, which the visitor will find on maps, road signs and city shopfronts, is known as *Pinyin*. It is now almost universally adopted by the Western media.

Some visitors may initially encounter some difficulty in pronouncing Romanized Chinese words. In fact many of the sounds correspond to the usual pronunciation of the letters in English. The exceptions are:

Initials

c	is like the *ts* in 'it*s*'
q	is like the *ch* in '*cheese*'
x	has no English equivalent, and can best be described as a hissing consonant that lies somewhere between *sh* and *s*. The sound was rendered as *hs* under an earlier transcription system.
z	is like the *ds* in 'fa*ds*'
zh	is unaspirated, and sounds like the *j* in '*jug*'.

Finals

a	sounds like '*ah*'
e	is pronounced as in '*her*'
i	is pronounced as in '*ski*' (written as *yi* when not preceded by an initial consonant). However, in *ci, chi, ri, shi, zi* and *zhi*, the sound represented by the final is quite different and is similar to the *ir* in '*sir*' but without much stressing of the *r* sound.
o	sounds like the *aw* in '*law*'
u	sounds like the *oo* in '*ooze*'
ü	is pronounced as the German *ü* (written as *yu* when not preceded by an initial consonant). The *ê* and *ū* are usually written simply as *e* and *u*.

Finals in Combination

When two or more finals are combined, such as in *hao, jiao* and *liu*, each letter retains its sound value as indicated in the list above, but note the following:

ai	is like the *ie* in 'tie'
ei	is like the *ay* in 'bay'
ian	is like the *ien* in 'Vienna'
ie	similar to 'ear'
ou	is like the *o* in 'code'
uai	sounds like 'why'
uan	is like the *uan* in 'iguana'
	(except when proceeded by *j, q, x* and *y*; in these cases a *u* following any of these four consonants is in fact *ü* and *uan* is similar to *uen*.)
ue	is like the *ue* in 'duet'
ui	sounds like 'way'

Examples

A few Chinese names are shown below with English phonetic spelling beside them:

Beijing	Bay-jing
Cixi	Tsi-shee
Guilin	Gway-lin
Hangzhou	Hahng-joe
Kangxi	Kahng-shee
Qianlong	Chien-loong
Tiantai	Tien-tie
Xian	Shee-ahn

An apostrophe is used to separate syllables in certain compound-character words to preclude confusion. For example, *Changan* (which can be *chang-an* or *chan-gan*) is sometimes written as *Chang'an*.

Tones

A Chinese syllable consists of not only an initial and a final or finals, but also a tone or pitch of the voice when the words are spoken. In *Pinyin* the four basic tones are marked ¯, ´, ˇ and `. These marks are almost never shown in printed form except in language texts.

Practical Information

Hotels

Xi'an did not have a Western-style hotel until the 1950s. In the early part of the century Chinese inns were open to foreigners, but many Western travellers arriving in Xi'an stayed with the European missionaries of the Scandinavian Alliance, the English Baptist Mission and the China Inland Mission.

Since the city's first joint-venture hotel, the Golden Flower, opened in 1985, many new international-standard hotels have been built. Now Xi'an has a surplus of quality accommodation, so that even in the peak seasons of spring and autumn many hotels still have a large percentage of their rooms vacant. In the winter, from mid-November until the end of March, these joint-venture hotels offer various bargain packages whereby tariffs are reduced, sometimes by up to 50 per cent. Check with individual hotels directly.

As elsewhere in China, hotels in Xi'an offer a confusing array of room classes and prices. Facilities in the average hotels for foreigners—those owned and run by the Chinese authorities—usually include air conditioning and heating, foreign exchange facility, telecommunications desk and souvenir shops. Many now accept the better-known credit cards. Most hotels can organize sightseeing tours to the major sights. The accommodation offered ranges from vast old-fashioned suites to modern, international-standard rooms. Standards of cleanliness and efficiency are equally varied.

SUPERIOR

Golden Flower Hotel (Jinhua Fandian)
8 Changle Xi Lu. Tel 332981; tlx 70145
GFH CN; fax 335477
金花饭店 长乐西路 8 号
500 rooms; US$95 + 10% service charge for a double room.
Opened in 1985, this is Xi'an's pioneer joint-venture hotel—and probably still the city's finest. Now expanded under a second phase of development, offering a comprehensive range of amenities and well-trained, attentive staff. Managed by SARA Hotels of Sweden.

Xi'an Garden Hotel (Tanghua Fandian)
4 Yanyin Lu (east of Big Goose Pagoda).
Tel 751111; tlx 70027 GAHTL CN; fax 751998
唐华饭店 大雁塔东侧雁引路 4 号
301 rooms; US$125 for a double room.
Tang-dynasty pavilion-style hotel, set amidst pools, rockeries and gardens in the shadow of the Big Goose Pagoda in the southern suburbs. Japanese joint-venture offering usual premier facilities, plus Tang Theatre-Restaurant and Tang Arts Museum.

Grand New World Hotel (Gudu Da Jiudian)
48 Lianhu Lu. Tel 716868; tlx 70156 XDHTL CN; fax 719754
古都新世界大酒店 莲湖路48号
501 rooms; US$80 + 15% service charge for standard double.
Located within the City Wall, west section, this hotel is run by World Hotel International and has comprehensive facilities and a 1130-seat theatre.

Hyatt Hotel (Kaiyue-Afanggong Fandian)
158 Dong Dajie. Tel 712020; tlx 70048 AFPH CN; fax 716799
西安凯悦（阿房宫）饭店 东大街158号
404 rooms; US$100 + 10% service charge for a double.
A luxury hotel associated with an international chain. Centrally located at a busy crossroads within the City Wall, close to the Bell Tower and Xi'an Railway Station.

Qin Dynasty Hotel (Qindu Jiudian)
55 Huancheng Xi Lu, Northern Section. Tel 719894; tlx 712718; fax 712728
秦都酒店 环城西路北段55号
181 rooms; US$65 for a double.
Newly opened four-star hotel, managed by China's International Hotels. Located at the West Gate of the City Wall.

Sheraton Xi'an Hotel (Xilaideng Jiudian)
12 Fenghao Lu. Tel 741888; tlx 70032 GAHL CN; fax 742188
喜来登酒店 丰镐路12号

480 rooms; US$70 + 10% service charge for a double room.
Representing one of over 500 Sheraton hotels, inns and resorts in 65 countries around the world, with usual luxury facilities. Outside the West Gate of the City Wall.

Grand Castle Hotel (Chang'an Chengbao Dajiudian)
South Gate. Tel 731860; fax 717926
长安国际酒店 南门外
Located just outside the South Gate, this hotel was scheduled to open in the winter of 1992. Managed by Japanese Airlines Group.

Royal Hotel, Xi'an
Dong Dajie. Tel 710305; fax 710795
西安皇城饭店 东大街
439 rooms; US$90 for a double.
Brand new hotel managed by Nikko Hotels International, providing the high standard of Japanese services. Located on busy Dong Dajie.

FIRST CLASS

Xi'an Guesthouse
26 Chang'an Lu. Tel 751351; tlx 70135 XAHTL CN; fax 751796
西安宾馆 长安北路26号
545 rooms; US$45 or FEC235 for a standard double.
A comfortable, medium-priced, Chinese-run hotel much favoured by package groups, close to the Little Goose Pagoda and CITS. Located just south of the City Wall.

Tangcheng Hotel
7 Lingyuan Nan Lu. Tel 751164/54171;
tlx 70013 TCH CN; fax 751041
唐城宾馆 陵园南路 7 号
406 rooms; US$46 for a double.
Opened in 1987. Medium-priced,
Chinese-run hotel with a Sky Bar on the
top of the 11-storey building, where you
can enjoy a bird's eye view of the city.
Located south of the City Wall.

Bell Tower Hotel (Zhonglou Fandian)
Southwest of the Bell Tower. Tel 29200;
tlx 70124; fax 718970
钟楼饭店 钟楼西南角
318 rooms; US$40 or FEC240 + 10%
service charge for a double.
Three-star. Good central location overlooking the Bell Tower and three minutes' walk from the Drum Tower and
Mosque. Under Holiday Inn manage-
ment, the hotel was recently refurnished.

Wannian Hotel
11 Changle Zhong Lu. Tel 331932;
tlx 70033 XWNH CN; fax 335460
万年饭店 长乐中路副11号
170 rooms; US$40 + 10% service charge
for a double.
Managed by a Hong Kong corporation.
Medium-priced and located east of the
City Wall.

Jianguo Hotel
20 Jinhua Nan Lu. Tel 338888;
tlx 700209 XAJGH CN; fax 335145
建国饭店 金花南路20号
843 rooms; US$65 + 10% service charge
for a double.

This Chinese-run, three-star hotel is
located east of the City Wall near the
Zoo. The building is a clone of Jianguo's
popular Beijing Hotel. Its Friendship
Shopping Mall is one of the best
shopping places in Xi'an.

Holiday Inn Xi'an
(Shenzhou Jiari Jiudian)
8 Huancheng Dong Lu. Tel 334311;
tlx 70043 COLT CN; fax 335962
神州假日酒店 环城东路南段 8 号
255 rooms; US$50 + 10% service charge
for a standard double.
Medium-priced, international-chain
hotel. Located at the southeast corner of
the City Wall, with great room views of
the Ming structure.

STANDARD

Xi'an People's Hotel (Renmin Dasha)
319 Dongxin Jie. Tel 715111;
tlx 710716 RMHTA CN; fax 718152
人民大厦 东新街319号
600 rooms; FEC120–180 for a double
room.
Reasonably priced and refurbished
Soviet-built hotel, with an excellent
location. Western and Chinese restaurants, bicycle rental, air-ticket office and
pleasant gardens.

City Hotel (Chengshi Jiudian)
5 Nan Dajie. Tel.719988; tlx 70042;
fax 716688
新世界酒店 南大街 5 号
138 rooms; FEC180 + 10% service
charge for a double room.

Shaanxi handicrafts on sale at the Qin Ling tombs

A joint-venture, reasonably priced hotel with a good central location.

Scarlet Bird Hotel (Zhuque Fandian)
26 Xiaozhai Xi Lu. Tel 752211;
tlx 70186; fax 751768
朱雀饭店 小寨西路26号
112 rooms; FEC186 (extended stays FEC145) for a double.
Reasonably priced Chinese-run hotel, close to the new Shaanxi History Museum, with a Silk Exhibition Hall.

Orient Hotel
26 Xiaozhai Xi Lu. Tel 752242;
tlx 700228 XAOH CN; fax 711768
东方大酒店 小寨西路26号
330 rooms. US$75 for a double.
New Chinese-run hotel, opened in July 1992. Close to the Shaanxi History Museum and the Big Goose Pagoda.

Jiefang Hotel
321 Jiefang Lu. Tel 28946; tlx 70044 XAJFH CN
解放饭店 解放路321号（西安火车站广场）
363 rooms; FEC99 for a standard double.
Recently redecorated Chinese-run hotel, directly outside the Xi'an Railway Station. Very reasonably priced.

China Merchants Hotel
(Huashang Jiudian)
131 Heping Lu. Tel 718988; tlx 700269 CMH CN; fax 718588
华商酒店 和平路131号
130 rooms; FEC200 for a double room.
Sino-Hong Kong joint-venture hotel.

Central location next to Hyatt Hotel. Medium-priced.

Hawaii Hotel (Xiaweiyi Jiudian)
54 Youyi Dong Lu. Tel 751288;
tlx 70198 XAHWH CN; fax 751128
夏威夷酒店 友谊东路56号
104 rooms; FEC118–148 for a double.
American joint-venture run by a Hong Kong hotel group, located south outside the City Wall.

Xiying Hotel (Xiying Da Jiudian)
70 Xiying Lu. Tel 55811; tlx 700213 FCHTL CN; fax 711585
西影大酒店 西影路70号
77 rooms; FEC132 for a standard double.
Run by Xi'an Film Studio, next to the Qin Palace and close to the Big Goose Pagoda.

Concord Hotel (Xiehe Fandian)
28 Fenghao Dong Lu. Tel 44460
协和饭店 丰镐路12号
160 rooms; FEC100–150 for a standard double.
A small Hong Kong joint-venture hotel.

BUDGET

May the First Hotel (Wuyi Fandian)
351 Dong Dajie. Tel 710804
五一饭店 东大街351号
70 rooms; RMB52.80 for a double.
City-centre location, with cheaply priced rooms. Chinese restaurant and a snack-shop just downstairs.

Yulan Hotel
40 Changle Xi Lu. Tel 335414;
cable 2171; fax 335639
榆兰饭店 长乐西路
200 beds; RMB80 for a double.
A small Chinese-owned and run hotel,
five minutes walk west from the Golden
Flower Hotel.

Victory Hotel (Shengli Fandian)
Yanta Lu. Tel 713184
胜利饭店 雁塔路
283 rooms; FEC100 for a double, rooms
with three beds for RMB60.
Very popular budget hotel located
outside the Heping Gate.

Shaanxi Institute of Mechanical Engineering Hotel
Jinhua Nan Lu. Tel 335656-532;
tlx 70047 SIME CN; fax 335545
陕西机械学院招待所 金花南路
24 rooms; RMB62.50 for a double.
Three minutes' walk from the Jiangou
Hotel, with some very cheap dormitory
accommodation—around RMB10 per
bed.

HOTELS OUTSIDE XI'AN

Huaqing Guesthouse
Lintong Country. Tel (09237) 2955
华清池宾馆 临潼县
23 rooms; RMB55 for a double.
Part of the hot springs, where you can
bathe. Near Terracotta Army Museum.

Qindu Hotel
5 Shengli Jie, Anding Lu, Xianyang.
Tel (0910) 5235
秦都饭店 咸阳市安定路胜利街 5 号
110 rooms; RMB55 for a double.
Located in Xianyang city centre 2
kilometres (1.2 miles) from the Xianyang Museum, which displays some
3,000 miniature Han terracotta warriors.

Huaxing Hotel
Qilizhen, Xingping County. Tel (09201)
22827; tlx 70079 HAWC CN
华兴宾馆 兴平县七里镇
55 rooms; FEC66 for a double.
Good location for touring to the
northwest of Xi'an, especially the Qian
Ling, Zhao Ling and Mao Ling
mausoleums; has a beautiful and
peaceful garden.

Restaurants

Jufengyuan Restaurant
151 Jiefang Lu. Tel 714863
聚丰园 解放路151号
Formerly called the Xi'an Sichuan Restaurant, this restaurant serves authentic Sichuanese food, which is characteristically hot and spicy and often includes whole garlic, chunks of tangy ginger and dried red chillies. Their 'Pock-marked Grandma Chen's Beancurd' (*Mapo doufu*) is named after the lady in Chengdu with a rough complexion who invented it.

May the First Restaurant
(Wuyi Fandian)
351 Dong Dajie. Tel 714410
五一饭店 东大街351号
This downtown hotel restaurant alongside the Foreign Language Bookstore is popular for banquets and provides local-style food. There are two snack restaurants on the first floor. Appropriately, the east one serves Chinese snack food such as *baozi* (steamed dumplings) and *wonton*. Some Western cakes and bread are served in the west section. It is open 8am–8pm.

Xi'an Restaurant (Heping Branch)
88 Heping Lu. Tel 714726
西安饭庄分店 和平路88号
This is the former Peace Restaurant, now reopened and serving Shaanxi-style dishes and local snack banquets. Its menu still includes Peace Restaurant specialities such as *chao babao* and

qinxiang shaomai. Open 10am–8.30pm.

Xi'an Restaurant (Xi'an Fanzhuang)
298 Dong Dajie. Tel 23821
西安饭庄 东大街298号
The largest restaurant in the city occupies a huge modern block with six floors containing 14 dining rooms. There is little discernible ambience. Food is officially Shaanxi style, and many of the delicacies, such as *kaoyangrou* and *yangrou shuijiao*, are available; however, the chefs are flexible and can cook other kinds of Chinese cuisine. The calligraphy of the sign in front of the building is by Guo Moruo, a literary eminence of the People's Republic.

East Asia Restaurant (Dongya Fandian)
46 Luoma Shi. Tel 718410
东亚饭庄 骡马市46号
All the chefs in this restaurant, which is near the Bell Tower on the bustling free market street of Luoma Shi, were originally from Shanghai, and officially they prepare the cuisine of Suzhou and Wuxi, cities in southern Jiangsu Province, close to Shanghai. Prices are reasonable and many dishes are delicious, especially *huashuiyu* (fish) and *xiangsuji* (double cooked crispy chicken). Open 8am–8pm.

Baiyunzhang Jiaozi Restaurant
Dong Dajie and Juhuayuan. Tel 719247
白云章饺子馆 东大街菊花园口
A Muslim restaurant which serves Hui-

Poster of the film Red Sorghum, *directed by Zhang Yimou*

style *jiaozi* (dumplings). Their speciality, a set of *jiaozi* (six different kinds including mutton, mushroom, seafood) is highly recommended. Open 10am–8pm.

Qingyazhai Restaurant
384 Dong Dajie. Tel 718268
清雅斋饭庄 东大街384号
This is also a Muslim restaurant run entirely by Hui, or Chinese Muslims. They specialize in lamb and vegetable dishes. Especially good are lamb *jiaozi*. It is on the south side of Dong Dajie, a little west of Dong Dajie Department Store going towards the Bell Tower.

New China Snacks
Dong Dajie
新中华 东大街
Between the Dong Dajie Department Store and the Qingyazhai Restaurant (see above), on the south side of the road, is a small but typical sweet snack shop. Everything is very cheap and the only way to order is to point. Fried glutinous rice, covered with sugar and containing red beans, is one favourite. Another is sweet congee, rice gruel in syrup with peanuts or *baihe*, lily bulb.

Jiefanglu Jiaozi Restaurant
229 Jiefang Lu. Tel 23185
解放路饺子馆 解放路229号
Located near the railway station, this is one of the best restaurants in town and is always packed with customers. It is advisable to book in advance. The total repertoire of the restaurant includes 125 varieties of dumpling (*jiaozi*) and other

speciality dishes which can be cooked on request.

A standard meal begins with excellent varied *hors d'oeuvres* which are then followed by 16 different varieties of dumpling. Some are fried and some are steamed; all are freshly cooked and go under exotic names such as 'Buddha's claw', 'concubine's dumpling' and 'make-money'. If you eat there on another day you may sample another 16 flavours. Dumpling meals are rounded off with a delicious chicken and duck 'dragon' soup served bubbling in a brass tureen over a burner, with miniature dumplings cooked in it at the table. There are more bowls of dumplings for anyone who is still hungry.

Tongshengxiang Paomo House
33 Xi Dajie. Tel 22170
同盛祥泡馍馆 西大街33号
A *paomo* and mutton hotpot banquet at this unpretentious restaurant is excellent value and is one of the most authentically Chinese experiences in town. On the edge of the Bell Tower Muslim quarter, the restaurant is well patronized by locals. The banquet menu includes varied *hors d'oeuvres* and traditional *paomo* (dry starchy bread broken into small pieces and submerged in hot, lightly spiced mutton broth), but the most highly recommended dish is a Mongolian-style hotpot cooked at the table. You hold the thinly sliced raw meat with chopsticks in the boiling water of the hotpot to cook it for a few seconds, then flavour it with a variety of sauces. This is

followed by 'dragon's moustache' soup, made with long rice noodles and vegetables. The restaurant is open 9am–7pm.

Defachang Jiaozi Restaurant
3 Xi Dajie. Tel 26453
德发长饺子馆 西大街 3 号
Located near the Bell Tower, this restaurant was opened in 1936. Beijing-style dumplings here are as attractive as the restaurant's name, 'Flourishing Virtues'. Many kinds of *jaozi* are tasty and served in a visually appealing way, such as 'Two Dragons playing with a Pearl' and 'All Flowers Exposed to the Sun'. Open 9am–8pm.

Small World
6 Heping Lu
小世界 和平路 6 号
Located just inside Heping Gate, this small private restaurant opened by one of the rapidly expanding entrepreneurial class serve Western breakfasts all day, as well as sandwiches, hamburgers and pizzas at reasonable prices. This is a good place to meet new friends who, perhaps like yourself, are having a taste of home in the middle of China. China guidebooks and magazines are provided for browsing.

Golden Flower Hotel Restaurants
8 Changle Xi Lu. Tel 332981
金花饭店 万福阁 玉泉轩 长乐西路 8 号
Wan Fu Court is regarded by the most critical of locals as the best restaurant in the city. The menu is predominantly Sichuanese but there are regional guest dishes. Some items on the menu are available only in season. Particularly recommended is the cold platter of poultry, bean curd (*doufu*) and beautifully sliced vegetables. Another delicious dish is Sichuan roast duck, a variation of the more famous Beijing counterpart. Alongside is the Western restaurant, the **Jade Spring**. Buffet breakfasts and dinners are good value, particularly for those travellers deprived of home cooking for a long time. In addition, for casual dining, there is a coffee shop which offers a variety of tasty dishes until the late hours.

Grand Metropolis Restaurant (Hongdu Jiujia)
3 Jinhua Lu
红都酒店 金花路 3 号
This Chinese and Western restaurant has a good menu of 'fast food', including hamburgers and sandwiches. It also offers a selection of pastries and desserts such as chocolate brownies, apple crumble and coconut macaroons. Located just north of the Jianguo Hotel.

Useful Addresses

TRAVEL SERVICES IN XI'AN

Overseas Travel Corporation, Shaanxi
15 Chang'an Bei Lu. Tel 751425
陕西海外旅游总公司 长安北路15号

Overseas Travel Corporation, Xi'an
158 Youyi Dong Lu. Tel 751530
西安海外旅游总公司 友谊东路158号

China International Travel Service, Xi'an Branch
32 Chang'an Bei Lu. Tel 752060
中国国际旅行社西安分社 长安北路32号

China Travel Service, Shaanxi
272 Jiefang Lu. Tel.712557
陕西省中国旅行社 解放路272号

China Youth Travel Service, Shaanxi
90 Hongying Lu. Tel. 712178
中国青年旅行社陕西分社 红缨路90号

TRANSPORTATION

Xianyang International Airport
Xianyang City. Tel 797872
咸阳国际机场 咸阳市

China Northwest Airlines Booking Office
296 Xishaomen (outside the West Gate). Tel 42264
中国西北民航售票处 西稍门296号

Shaanxi United Airlines Booking Office
319 Dong Xin Jie. Tel 715111
陕西航联售票处 东新街319号

Xi'an Customs
91 Zhujue Dajie. Tel 752332
西安海关 朱雀大街91号

Xi'an Bus Station
Xi'an Railway Station Square. Tel 713598
西安汽车站 火车站广场西南

Xi'an City Bus Station
Fengqing Lu. Tel 713616
西安市汽车站 丰庆路

Nanguan Bus Station
Huancheng Nan Lu Xi Duan (Western Section). Tel 712563
南关汽车站 环城南路西段

Yuxiang Gate Bus Station
Huancheng Xi Lu. Tel 712061
玉祥门汽车站 环城西路

Taxi Company No 1 Parking Area
Bell Tower. Tel 714759
出租汽车公司一场 钟楼

Taxi Company No 2 Parking Area
Railway Station. Tel 711497
出租汽车公司二场 火车站

Railway Station Ticket Office
Tel 712674
西安市火车站售票处 火车站东侧

(preceding page) The Big Goose pagoda

SHOPS

Jianguo Hotel Friendship Shopping Mall
20 Jinhua Nan Lu. Tel 338888
建国饭店友谊商场 金花南路20号

Xi'an Antique Store
375 Dong Dajie. Tel 715847
西安市文物商店 东大街375号

Ji Bao Art Treasures Store
14 Nanxin Jie. Tel 712085
集宝斋工艺品商店 南新街14号

Wenbaozhai Store
5 Yanta Zhong Lu. Tel 751607
Xi'an Friendship Store
1 Nanxin Jie. Tel 713898
西安文宝斋商场 雁塔路中段 5 号

Shaanxi shadow puppet

Xi'an International Store, Da Cien Temple Branch
Inside the Big Goose Pagoda. Tel 53802
西安国际商场大慈恩寺分店 大雁塔内

Xi'an Special Arts & Crafts Factory
138 Huancheng Xi Lu Bei Duan (Northern Section). Tel 43128
西安市特种工艺美术厂 环城西路北段138号

National Folk Art Gallery
16 Yanta Lu. Tel 51602
民族民间美术馆 雁塔路16号

Foreign Languages Bookstore, Shaanxi Province
349 Dong Dajie. Tel 24414, 22197
陕西省外文书店 东大街349号

Tangcheng Department Store
Dong Dajie. Tel 710666
唐城百货大厦 东大街

Minsheng Department Store
103 Jiefang Lu. Tel 717665
民生百货商店 解放路103号

OTHERS

Bank of China, Shaanxi Branch
233 Jiefang Lu. Tel 22312
中国银行陕西分行 解放路233号

Bank of China, Xi'an Branch
52 Honghui Xiang, Tanshi Jie.
Tel 710069
中国银行西安分行 炭市街红会巷52号

Long-distance Telecommunication Office, Xi'an City
Xixin Jie. Tel 24007
西安长途电信局 西新街

Post Office, Xi'an City
1 Bei Dajie. Tel 27555
西安市邮政局 北大街1号

Shaanxi Province Travel Bureau, Office for Tourist Complaints
15 Chang'an Bei Lu. Tel 751148, (8 am–6 pm) Mandarin and English
陕西省旅游局旅游举报办公室 长安北路15号

Commission of Foreign Trade, Shaanxi Province
Xincheng. Tel 791642
陕西省对外贸易局 新城

Foreign Affairs Office, People's Government of Shaanxi Province
272 Jiefang Lu. Tel 710309
陕西省人民政府外事办公室 解放路272号

Shaanxi Provincial Hospital
19 Youyi Xi Lu. Tel 51331, 53261
陕西省医院 友谊西路19号

Fourth Army Hospital
Changle Lu. Tel 332971, 331741
第四军医大学医院 长乐路

Division of Aliens and Entry-Exit Administration of the Xi'an Municipal Public Security Bureau
138 Xi Dajie. Tel 25121
西安市公安局出入境管理处 西大街138号

Index of Places